Man Up

Conquering the Mother Wound to
Forge Authentic Relationships

Marie Benjamin

Table of Contents

Preface — 3
Chapter 1: Unraveling the Mother Bond — 6
    The Mother of All Bonds: Where It All Begins — 8
    Understanding the Influence of Maternal Relationships — 11
Chapter 2: Embracing Vulnerability: The First Step — 21
Chapter 3: Beyond Isolation: Finding Your Tribe — 35
    Who Said You Have to Go It Alone? — 38

Chapter 4: The Holistic Healing Handbook — 50
    Unpacking the Toolbox: A Guide to Holistic Healing — 53
Chapter 5: The Mirror of Self-Awareness — 67
    Unveiling the Hidden Threads: How Your Mother's Influence Shapes You — 69
    Understanding the Impact of Maternal Wounds on Thoughts and Behaviors — 71
Chapter 7: The Art of Boundary Setting — 92
Chapter 8: Conversations that Heal — 108
Chapter 9: Leaning on Trustworthy Shoulders — 121
Chapter 10: Reclaiming the Narrative: A New Dawn — 135
    Reclaim Your Story, Redefine Your Bonds — 139
    Epilogue: Writing the Next Chapter — 144
    Activity: The Letter to Yourself — 146
    One Final Prompt — 148

Preface

"You can't separate peace from freedom because no one can be at peace unless he has his freedom." — Malcolm X

As I prepared to write this preface, the powerful words of Malcolm X echoed in my mind. "You can't separate peace from freedom because no one can be at peace unless he has his freedom." This book, at its heart, is about finding that peace. It's about liberating oneself from the unseen chains that past relationships with maternal figures may have subtly, yet powerfully, bound around one's capacity for intimacy and connection.

It's a journey of stepping out of the shadows of emotional pain and trauma, and into the light of healing, self-awareness, and emotional resilience.

This book seeks to untangle the complicated emotions men often face as they strive to understand and recover from maternal wounds. It's not just a tale of confronting the past—it's about making sense of it. Understanding why the emotional stains are there and finding practical ways to wash them clean and prevent new ones. Through a blend of personal reflections, psychological wisdom, and practical tools, this book offers a path for men ready to explore their inner world and foster healthier relationships with themselves and others.

My motivation to write this book sprang from witnessing many men around me, struggling silently with their emotional baggage. Men who excel in their careers and social lives but can't seem to maintain a lasting romantic relationship or they feel inexplicably hollow despite their successes. These are not just random scenarios; they are real-life challenges faced by real people. Their battles and their bravery in confronting what many would rather sweep under the rug inspired me to delve deeper into this issue.

In crafting this narrative, I drew heavily from psychological research and therapeutic practices but also from the vibrant stories shared by men who have dared to tread this path. Their journeys underscore not only the prevalence of the issue but also the profound impact that healing can have on one's life.

I am immensely grateful for every story shared with me, every professor who lent their insight, and everyone who supported me through this journey.

To you, dearest reader—thank you for your courage and curiosity. You're not just reading a book; you're stepping into a community that is dedicated to growth and emotional clarity. Whether you've felt misunderstood or isolated in your experiences, or you're simply seeking deeper self-awareness and healthier relationships, you've found your squad here.

There's no prerequisite knowledge needed —just an open mind and the willingness to dive deep into your emotional world.

As we turn these pages together, remember: this journey is not just about confronting past pains but also about crafting a future rich with authentic relationships and unshakeable self-esteem. So lace up your boots; it's time to walk this path of healing and empowerment together.

And with that said, keep turning these pages—your answers (and new beginnings) lie just ahead.

Chapter 1: Unraveling the Mother Bond

James stood at the edge of the playground, his gaze fixed on the jubilant chaos of children swirling around swings and slides. His daughter, Maya, with her bright red coat and pigtails, was a vibrant splash against the drabness of late autumn. She laughed, a sound that seemed to pierce through the crisp air straight into James's heart. He remembered that laugh; it was her mother's.

As James watched Maya play, he found himself grappling with an old, gnawing feeling—a mixture of admiration and a deep-seated fear. His relationship with his own mother had been a complex ball of warmth shadowed by stern expectations. She had been his first encounter with love and also with criticism. Now, as a father, these memories shaped his every interaction with his little girl.

The park was mostly empty, save for a few parents clustered in twos and threes, their breath forming clouds as they talked. James felt like an outsider among them. He often wondered if his own emotional reserves were enough to foster in Maya a healthy sense of self and others. The thought was like a weight, pressing down on him with each of her delighted squeals.

He recalled how after a stern reprimand or outburst, his mother would draw him close with a hug , with food , a treat, or a trip to his favorite store. This gesture, meant to divert his attention to something more joyous, served as a tacit admission of guilt. However, it just created confusion for James, who struggled to understand the conflicting emotions of affection and discipline. This dance of push and pull left a lasting impact on his relationships, leading him to question whether affection could exist without underlying conditions.

A shout from Maya broke his reverie as she beckoned him over to help her climb the tall slide. As he lifted her up, feeling the trust in her small hands gripping his fingers tightly, he realized this was what it all boiled down to—trust.

Was he doing enough? Was he doing it right? These questions haunted him more than he cared to admit.

Walking back home as dusk began to paint the sky in shades of orange and purple, James pondered how deeply our beginnings are tied to our endings—how the emotional blueprint laid down by our earliest relationships shapes everything that follows.

Maya skipped alongside him, humming a tune under her breath—a simple moment so full of life and possibility.

Could understanding his past give James the insight needed to guide Maya toward a future where she felt secure in herself and her relationships? How much does our childhood shape our ability to love and be loved?

The Mother of All Bonds: Where It All Begins

When it comes to unpacking the luggage we carry into our adult relationships, few things weigh us down, quite like unresolved issues with our mothers. It's not just about whether you had enough hugs as a kid; this is about how these foundational experiences shape your entire approach to connecting with others. In this first chapter, we dive deep into understanding how maternal relationships influence your perception of self and others. It's essential groundwork for anyone ready to challenge their emotional status quo and foster healthier connections.

For many men, the relationship with their mother is the first mirror reflecting who they are in the world. If that reflection is warped by neglect, overbearing attitudes, or inconsistent affection, it distorts how a man sees himself and, subsequently, how he interacts with the world. Recognizing this can be tough – it requires peeling back layers of bravado or detachment that many have built up as armor.

Understanding the role of a mother's bond doesn't mean blaming mom for everything that's gone wrong in your life; rather, it's about acknowledging her role in your emotional blueprint. This blueprint shapes not only your sense of self-worth but also how you form attachments and manage relationships in adulthood. Whether it's trust issues, fear of commitment, or a pattern of emotional unavailability, these threads can often be traced back to those early interactions.

In exploring these themes, we're not just indulging in a blame game but rather setting the stage for **profound healing**. By identifying personal emotional challenges rooted in maternal relationships, you empower yourself to start rewriting your narrative. This isn't about rewriting history but about understanding it well enough to move forward without its chains.

This chapter sets the foundation for what lies ahead: a journey toward authentic connections that are both enriching and sustaining. The insights here pave the way for later discussions on overcoming barriers to intimacy and vulnerability—key ingredients in any genuine relationship.

The path to healing is not linear and requires patience and resilience. It involves confronting uncomfortable truths and dismantling defensive walls built over years. However, the rewards of such endeavors are immeasurable. Imagine forming relationships where you feel understood and valued—not for the mask you wear but for who you truly are beneath it.

To all my brothers out there grappling with these issues, know this: ***understanding is the first step toward change.*** Armed with insights from this chapter, you're better equipped to tackle the emotional legwork needed to heal and thrive in your relationships.

Embrace this knowledge not just as a critique of past pains but as a beacon guiding you toward deeper connections and a more fulfilled self. Let's get to work on building those bridges—first within ourselves and then with others around us.

Understanding the Influence of Maternal Relationships

Our relationships with our mothers can deeply influence the way we see ourselves and interact with others. From the moment a baby locks eyes with their mother, an imprint is made that forms the blueprint of their self-perception and their expectations from relationships. This initial connection, rich with silent understandings and unspoken agreements, sets the stage for how we will engage with the world.

Mothers are often our first teachers in the school of emotional expression and regulation. They model behaviors that children, consciously or subconsciously, learn to emulate. If a mother consistently demonstrates warmth and responsiveness, her child is likely to develop a secure attachment style. This means feeling confident in both self-worth and in trusting others. Conversely, if the maternal figure is distant or erratic in affection, it can foster insecurity and difficulty in forming close bonds later in life.

Imagine a young tree growing in fertile soil with ample sunlight compared to one trying to sprout under a dense canopy. The former flourishes uninhibited while the latter struggles for every bit of nutrients and light. Similarly, children nurtured with consistent love and support from their mothers are like trees planted in rich soil, likely to grow strong and resilient. Those who experience less attentive care may constantly feel they are competing for emotional sustenance.

The subtleties of this influence are profound. They shape not just whom we connect with but how we interpret these connections. It's about more than being liked or disliked; it's about understanding respect, trust, boundaries, and affection. These early interactions send ripples across the pond of life, affecting all future relationships.

Mothers profoundly shape our view of ourselves and our interactions with others.

The Foundational Role of the Mother-Child Bond

The relationship between a mother and her child serves as the cornerstone upon which future relationships are built. This foundational bond informs much about an individual's approach to relationships — be it friendships, romantic involvement, or professional associations.

Research underscores that children who experience secure attachments with their mothers typically exhibit healthier relationship patterns in adulthood. These individuals often find it easier to form stable, trusting relationships because they learned these dynamics during their formative years. They tend to believe that people are generally reliable and that close relationships provide a source of comfort and support.

On the flip side, those who have experienced insecure attachments might struggle more significantly. They might perceive relationships as unreliable sources of support or even as potential threats to their emotional well-being. Such views can lead to patterns of avoidance or anxiety regarding closeness and intimacy.

Let's consider communication as a dance where each participant learns their steps from those who danced before them — primarily from parents or caregivers. If a child sees open communication modeled by a nurturing mother, they're likely to adopt similar patterns themselves. However, if communication within this bond is fraught with misunderstanding or conflict, these patterns can repeat themselves in later life.

This understanding helps us recognize why some individuals might repeatedly encounter issues in forming or maintaining healthy relationships despite their best efforts. It isn't merely about making better choices or trying harder; sometimes it's about unlearning deeply ingrained ways of relating that trace back to the earliest days of mother-child interactions.

How might your current relationship challenges be echoes of your earliest experiences with your mother?

Identifying Emotional Challenges Rooted in Maternal Relationships

Personal emotional challenges often find their roots deep within our earliest experiences with our mothers. Recognizing this link can be transformative in understanding oneself better and paving the way for significant personal growth.

Consider emotions as colors on an artist's palette: The initial set of colors available to us comes from our first home environment — predominantly shaped by maternal influence. If a child grows up seeing a broad spectrum of healthy emotional expression from their mother, they likely feel confident using a wide range of emotional 'colors' themselves. Conversely, if they see only limited expressions — perhaps shades of anger or sadness dominate — this, too, shapes their emotional repertoire.

For many men especially, untangling these early emotional lessons can be challenging yet crucial for personal development and relational success. It's not uncommon for men to feel pressure to suppress vulnerable emotions perceived as weak or unmasculine – often mirroring societal cues possibly reinforced by family dynamics starting from childhood.

By revisiting these formative experiences through reflection or therapy, one can start disentangling what emotions were deemed acceptable and which were suppressed or ignored within their maternal relationship dynamic. This exploration can illuminate recurring emotional patterns and trigger points in current relationships.

Understanding how maternal bonds influence perception allows us to recognize the fundamental roles these relationships play in shaping future connections and identify personal emotional challenges rooted therein

Through this opening chapter, we've embarked on a profound exploration of how our very first relationship—the one with our mothers—casts long, influential shadows over our self-perception and our interactions with others. **Understanding the mother bond** is like unlocking a map to your emotional DNA—tracing back to where your feelings, reactions, and relationships begin.

Remember, guys, it's not just about digging into past emotional entanglements. It's about sculpting the future ones with intention and wisdom. By recognizing how these early experiences shape us, we can reroute our journey toward more fulfilling and authentic connections. It's like recalibrating your emotional compass so you're no longer navigating through fog but moving forward with clear skies.

As we step into the subsequent chapters, brace yourselves for an exhilarating ride into deeper self-awareness. We'll unravel strategies that not only help you understand the nuances of your emotions but also equip you with tools to heal and transform those wounds into sources of strength. *Imagine transforming scars into superpowers*—how empowering is that?

Each page you turn will bring you closer to redefining resilience and fostering relationships that aren't just about survival but about thriving. This isn't just a journey; it's an upgrade to your emotional blueprint.

So let's keep that momentum! The insights you gain here are just the beginning—a foundation for stronger, healthier connections that honor both your past and your potential for growth. Together, we'll continue to uncover the layers of our experiences and stride confidently towards a horizon of emotional freedom and robust health.

The Different Faces of the Mother Wound: Know Thy Enemy

Alright, gentlemen, let's get down to brass tacks. We've talked about the mother wound in general, but it's not a one-size-fits-all kind of deal. It comes in different flavors, each leaving its own unique mark on your emotional landscape. Recognizing which one you're dealing with is like identifying the enemy in battle—crucial for strategizing your way to victory.

1. **The Neglectful Mother Wound:**

   This one's a classic. It stems from a lack of emotional or physical nurturing during your formative years. Maybe your mom was physically present but emotionally distant, or perhaps she was just plain MIA. Either way, this wound can leave you feeling like you're constantly craving love and validation, yet never quite feeling full. It can manifest as trust issues, fear of intimacy, and a nagging sense of unworthiness that whispers, "You're not good enough."

2. **The Overbearing Mother Wound:**

   On the flip side, we have the overbearing mother—the one who hovers like a helicopter, micromanages your every move, and criticizes more than she compliments. This type of wound can leave you feeling suffocated and doubting your own abilities. It can manifest as perfectionism, people-pleasing tendencies, and a constant need for external approval. You might find yourself saying "yes" when you really want to scream "no," all because you're terrified of disappointing others.

3. **The Inconsistent Mother Wound:**

   This one's a real mind-bender. It comes from a mother whose love and affection were unpredictable—hot one minute, cold the next. This emotional rollercoaster can leave you feeling anxious, insecure, and constantly on edge. You might find yourself second-guessing everything, always waiting for the other shoe to drop. It can also lead to a pattern of seeking out drama and chaos in relationships, as that's what feels familiar.

4. **The Narcissistic Mother Wound:**

   Here we've got the mother who saw you as an extension of herself, rather than your own person. Her needs always took center stage, and your feelings were left to fend for themselves. Growing up under this shadow can lead to low self-esteem, an inability to set boundaries, and a tendency to seek validation through overachievement—or in extreme cases, shutting down entirely. You might find yourself in relationships where you replay this dynamic, always giving and rarely receiving.

5. **The Critical Mother Wound:**

   This is the mother whose words cut deep, whether

they were meant to or not. If you grew up hearing "You'll never amount to anything" or "Why can't you be like so-and-so," you might have internalized those messages as your own truth. The result? A relentless inner critic that picks apart everything you do. This wound can manifest as anxiety, perfectionism, and an inability to celebrate your own accomplishments.

6. The Abandoning Mother Wound:

Whether she left physically, emotionally, or both, the abandoning mother leaves a profound void. This wound teaches you early on that love isn't guaranteed—it's conditional, fleeting, and often out of reach. As a result, you might fear abandonment in your adult relationships, holding on too tightly or pushing people away before they can hurt you. Trust issues are a hallmark of this wound, as is the deep-seated belief that you're not worth staying for.

7. The Enmeshed Mother Wound:

Here's the mother who blurred the lines between your identity and hers. She leaned on you emotionally, turning you into her confidant, partner, or even her parent. While this might have felt like closeness at the time, it often leads to an inability to set boundaries and a fear of being alone. You might struggle with asserting your independence or even recognizing your own desires, as they were often overshadowed by hers.

Here's the deal: these wounds don't just disappear on their own. They can linger in the shadows, sabotaging your relationships and hindering your personal growth. But recognizing them is the first step toward healing. It's like shining a spotlight on the enemy, revealing their weaknesses and giving you the upper hand.

So, take a good look in the mirror, fellas. Which of these wounds resonates with you? Once you know what you're dealing with, you can start crafting a battle plan for recovery. The journey won't be easy, but with each step, you reclaim a piece of yourself—and that, my friends, is worth the fight.

Chapter 2: Embracing Vulnerability: The First Step

In the hush of early morning, Michael sat alone on the worn-out bench in the corner of Jackson Park, a place that often served as his refuge when the weight of his thoughts needed room to expand. The crisp Chicago air brushed against his cheeks, a gentle reminder that seasons change just as people do. He watched as leaves, tinged with autumn's first kiss, fluttered to the ground, each descent a quiet ballet of surrender.

Michael had always been the rock in his family—the steadfast one who didn't show weakness. But lately, he found himself wrestling with memories of his mother that shaped so much of who he was but also held him back. It was an odd thing to consider vulnerability not just as a fleeting state but as a strength. As he sat there, the sound of distant traffic melding with the rustling trees, he thought about how showing his true feelings might be the first step toward healing.

His phone buzzed in his pocket—a message from his brother asking how he was doing. Normally, Michael would reply with a standard "I'm good," but today felt different. His thumb hovered over the keyboard as he considered whether to share more of his real struggles. Could admitting that he wasn't always strong be what would ultimately make him stronger?

He remembered a conversation with an old friend from college who had opened up about going to therapy after dealing with grief. Michael had admired his courage but never thought it was something he could do himself—until now. The stigma around men talking about their feelings was like an invisible barrier that kept him confined in silent battles.

The park began to fill slowly; joggers nodded at him in silent camaraderie as they passed by. Each nod seemed like an unspoken acknowledgment of shared struggles—each person fighting some unseen battle beneath their calm exteriors.

With a deep breath that felt like it reached down into the depths of his soul, Michael typed out a response to his brother that was more honest than any he had sent before: "Actually, I've been having a tough time lately. Thinking about getting some help." He hit send before doubt could reclaim him.

As he watched another leaf break free and drift toward the earth—a silent act of bravery—he wondered if this moment might be remembered as when everything started to change for him.

Would others see this admission not as weakness but as an act of courage? Would they understand that healing begins where pretense ends?

Who Said Real Men Don't Cry?

Let's cut straight to the chase: vulnerability isn't just some buzzword your therapist throws around to see you squirm. It's the real deal in healing, especially when you're wrestling with a maternal wound that's been messing with your head and heart. The journey to patching up those emotional scars begins with letting your guard down, which, believe it or not, takes more guts than keeping it up.

In a world where men are often boxed into the "strong, silent type," showing any form of emotional openness can feel like stepping into a spotlight wearing nothing but your truths. However, this chapter isn't just about airing out your dirty laundry for everyone to see. It's about understanding that **vulnerability is a strength**, not a weakness. It's the first step in acknowledging that something inside needs attention—a kind of bravery that many might never dare to show.

Society has had its say—now it's your turn. For too long, men have been fed the narrative that emotions are for the weak. But here's a hot take: maybe those old-school norms are the real weak links here. Overcoming this stigma isn't just liberating; it's revolutionary. By redefining what it means to be vulnerable, you're not only challenging an outdated status quo but also paving a path toward genuine emotional wellness.

Now, adopting vulnerability doesn't mean you've got to spill your guts at every turn. Think of it more like becoming fluent in a new language—the language of self-awareness and emotional growth. It's about getting real with yourself so you can heal properly. This isn't just touchy-feely talk; it's about building a foundation for stronger, more authentic connections with others and, most importantly, with yourself.

So how do you start? First, by recognizing that vulnerability is not about weakness but about facing up to your truths—however uncomfortable they may be. It's like stepping into the gym for the first rep of a heavyweight session; daunting at first, but incredibly rewarding as you progress.

Let's Get Practical

Alright, fellas, let's get real. Embracing vulnerability isn't about diving headfirst into an ocean of feelings or suddenly becoming the guy who shares his life story at happy hour. It's about small, intentional steps that build emotional strength over time—like hitting the gym for your heart and mind. Here's how you start flexing that muscle:

Step 1: Catch Yourself in the Act

First things first, start paying attention to the moments when you're most tempted to shut down emotionally. You know the ones—when someone asks, "What's wrong?" and you immediately respond with "I'm fine," even though you're anything but. Hit pause. Ask yourself, what am I really afraid of here? Nine times out of ten, it's not the judgment of others that's got you locked up—it's that internal critic shouting things like, "Don't be weak" or "No one cares." Recognizing this is half the battle.

Step 2: Test the Waters in Safe Spaces

Now, don't go spilling your guts to the first stranger you meet. Vulnerability is like learning to swim—you start in the shallow end. Find a trusted friend, a mentor, or even a professional counselor where you can start practicing opening up. Begin with something manageable, like sharing what's been stressing you out at work or what you've been feeling about a recent life event. And yes, it's okay to dip a toe into those deeper waters, like those unresolved feelings about mom.

Here's the kicker: it's not about getting it perfect. It's about showing up. Think of it like building your bench press—you don't start with 250 pounds on the bar. You start with the bar itself, then gradually add more weight. Every conversation, every moment of openness, adds another plate.

Step 3: Celebrate the Wins

We're conditioned to think that progress only counts if it's massive. But when it comes to emotional growth, the small wins are the game-changers. Did you open up about your frustration today without letting it boil over into anger? That's a win. Did you ask for help with something instead of bottling it up? Another step forward.

Track these moments, even if it's just mentally. Treat them like personal milestones. You wouldn't dismiss the first 10 pounds you lost in the gym just because you're not at your goal weight yet, right? Same rules apply here. Recognizing and celebrating these small victories will keep you motivated to keep going.

Step 4: Build Emotional Resilience with Action

Vulnerability isn't just about talking—it's also about doing. Show your emotional strength through small acts of bravery. Apologize when you've messed up, even if it makes your stomach turn. Take responsibility for your actions instead of deflecting. Be present when someone else opens up to you, even if you're not sure what to say. These actions don't just build connections—they reinforce the idea that you're capable of showing up as your true self.

Step 5: Keep It in Perspective

Here's the deal: vulnerability isn't about being soft—it's about being real. It's about saying, "I'm human, and that's okay." The irony is, when you embrace vulnerability, you don't lose respect—you gain it, starting with yourself. Think about the men you admire. Chances are, they're not the ones who pretend to have it all figured out—they're the ones who own their struggles and keep moving forward anyway.

This isn't a one-and-done kind of deal. Vulnerability is a lifelong practice. But the more you lean in, the more you'll see how it transforms your relationships, your confidence, and your sense of self. So start small, stay consistent, and don't be afraid to stumble along the way. Because every step forward, no matter how small, is proof that you're in the fight—and that's what really counts.

Wrapping It Up With Swag

Look at vulnerability as your secret weapon—an invisible tool belt equipped with everything you need for deep emotional healing and building badass authentic relationships. So let down those walls (gradually, of course), and step into a space where real growth happens. Trust me; it's worth every awkward moment and tough conversation.

Remember: **Real strength comes from facing what scares us**—and nothing says "I got this" like turning the key to unlock your deepest feelings and stepping through whatever comes out on the other side. Now go ahead and flex that vulnerability muscle—it looks good on you!

Reframe Vulnerability as a Strength Necessary for Healing

Vulnerability often carries a heavy stigma, especially among men. It's seen not as a strength but as a sign of weakness, something to be concealed rather than embraced. Yet, the truth is quite the opposite. Embracing vulnerability is a fundamental step in healing from deep-seated wounds, including those inflicted by maternal relationships.

Imagine vulnerability as the necessary opening of a tightly sealed jar. Without that initial twist, you can't access what's inside. Similarly, without opening up about our feelings and experiences, we block access to the kind of introspection and external support needed for healing. This opening is not just about airing out what's inside; it's about letting in light and fresh air to start the cleansing process.

Research supports this shift in perspective. Studies show that individuals who practice vulnerability are better at managing stress and anxiety, leading to improved overall well-being. Moreover, vulnerability allows for deeper connections with others, fostering relationships that provide support and understanding—key components in any healing journey.

However, embracing vulnerability requires courage. It demands facing the fears of judgment and rejection head-on. But remember, the strength it takes to be vulnerable is the very strength that pushes your healing forward. It's about being honest with yourself and others about your needs and experiences. **_Vulnerability is not weakness; it's the gateway to emotional liberation and strength._**

Overcome the Societal Stigma Associated with Male Vulnerability

Society often dictates that men should be stoic and unyielding. From a young age, boys hear admonitions like "Boys don't cry" or "Man up," embedding a sense of shame around expressing vulnerability. This societal conditioning can make it extremely challenging for men to express their emotions healthily and openly.

But let's break down these barriers with some hard facts: Emotional repression contributes significantly to mental health issues such as depression and anxiety. The pressure to conform to traditional masculine norms can exacerbate feelings of isolation and inadequacy when dealing with personal traumas or emotional struggles.

Why then do we cling to these outdated norms? Partly because they are self-perpetuating. When everyone around you seems to adhere to these standards, stepping out of that line feels risky—like standing alone in an open field during a storm. Yet, here lies the paradox: it's only when you step out that you find others who feel the same way, ready to stand alongside you.

Consider this: embracing vulnerability might initially feel like walking into a cold sea—the shock hits you first, but soon it becomes invigorating, empowering even. By showing your true self, you give permission for others to do the same, potentially leading a change in societal views on masculinity.

What would happen if more men viewed showing their true selves not as a risk but as a revolution?

Adopt Vulnerability as a Tool for Self-awareness and Emotional Growth

Vulnerability is more than just an emotional outlet; it's a powerful tool for self-awareness. It allows us to look inwardly with honesty about our feelings and experiences without judgment. This introspection is crucial for personal growth and healing from past wounds.

When you allow yourself to be vulnerable, you start noticing patterns in your behavior and reactions that may stem from unresolved issues or past traumas—like how certain comments trigger disproportionate anger or how certain people make you feel insecure.

Using vulnerability this way turns it into an active tool in your emotional toolkit—not just something that happens to you but something you wield deliberately to clear your path towards healing. Think of it like pruning a garden; cutting back overgrown branches encourages healthy growth.

Incorporating regular practices such as mindfulness or journaling can facilitate this process by providing structured ways to explore your vulnerabilities safely and constructively. These practices help articulate feelings that might otherwise remain nebulous clouds hanging over your psyche.

By adopting vulnerability consciously, we transform it into a catalyst for growth and resilience, integrating our experiences into our broader understanding of ourselves and our world.

Embracing vulnerability opens us up not only to personal growth but also fosters deeper connections with others—a true strength in disguise, capable of transforming societal perceptions and enhancing our own emotional well-being simultaneously.

Vulnerability isn't just a buzzword; it's the secret sauce to genuine healing and emotional growth. We've unpacked how seeing vulnerability as a strength, not a weakness, can revolutionize our approach to healing those deep-seated maternal wounds. Let's face it, society hasn't been too kind on men who show their soft sides, but here's the kicker: it's precisely that soft side that holds the key to profound self-awareness and connection.

Breaking free from societal stigmas is no small feat. It demands courage and a hefty dose of resilience. Remember, every time you choose to be open about your struggles, you're not just healing yourself; you're paving the way for a brother, a friend, or even a stranger to feel safe enough to share their own stories. That's how powerful your truth can be.

Adopting vulnerability as a tool isn't just about getting in touch with your feelings—it's about transforming them into stepping stones towards a healthier, more aware version of yourself. Think of it as upgrading your internal software. Every moment you choose to be vulnerable, you're debugging years of emotional glitches that have kept you from your true potential.

And let's get real—this journey isn't just about facing what's uncomfortable; it's about embracing it with open arms and maybe even a cheeky grin. It's about saying, "Yes, this hurts. Yes, this is tough. But I'm tougher." It's in these moments that we find our true spirit—unbroken and resilient.

So, as we wrap up this chapter, remember: *your vulnerability is your strength.* Harness it. Own it. Use it to fuel your journey towards healing and authentic connections. The road might be bumpy, but the destination? It's worth every step. Here's to turning those emotional scars into symbols of victory and wisdom!

Chapter 3: Beyond Isolation: Finding Your Tribe

Marcus walked down the familiar streets of his childhood neighborhood, the late afternoon sun spilling golden light over weathered houses and chain-link fences. The laughter of children echoed through the air, punctuated by the occasional bark of a dog or the distant hum of a lawnmower. His footsteps fell into a steady rhythm on the cracked pavement, a comforting metronome to the swirl of thoughts in his mind.

The streets hadn't changed much—at least not the way Marcus had. As a kid, these sidewalks had been his playground, a place of scraped knees, carefree bike rides, and unrelenting imagination. Back then, the world seemed full of possibility. But adulthood had brought with it a weight he couldn't shake.

Marcus had spent years running—not in the physical sense, but from a pain buried deep inside him. The maternal wound, as he'd come to call it, wasn't a loud, screaming kind of pain.

It was quiet, insidious, a shadow that whispered doubts and fears in his most vulnerable moments. He had tried everything to silence it: self-help books, solitary reflection, gritting his teeth and pushing forward. Yet the ache lingered, always just out of reach, like an itch he couldn't quite scratch.

Today, as he passed Mrs. Thompson's old bakery—its windows boarded up and its paint peeling—he was struck by a bittersweet memory. Mrs. Thompson used to offer him a warm slice of pound cake and a hug that felt like sunshine after school. For a brief moment, her kindness had filled the gaps his mother's distance left behind. Marcus felt a pang of loss, not just for Mrs. Thompson but for the sense of community he hadn't realized he'd been missing.

The thought hit him hard: healing wasn't something he could do alone. He had spent so much time trying to patch himself up in isolation, yet the moments that had brought him the most peace—the ones that made him feel whole, even if only briefly—had always involved others.

He rounded the corner to the park, where life hummed with quiet joy. A group of kids were engaged in a heated game of basketball, their shouts carrying on the breeze. Nearby, a family gathered around a picnic table, laughing over a shared meal. The scene pulled at something deep within him, something he hadn't felt in a long time.

Marcus slowed his pace, watching from the edge of the park. The simplicity of these connections—parents handing out sandwiches, friends ribbing each other over missed shots—felt profound. He realized he craved that kind of belonging, that kind of shared experience. But admitting it, and acting on it, was another matter. Vulnerability wasn't just foreign to him; it was terrifying.

As he turned to leave, Mrs. Johnson's voice called out from her porch, cutting through his thoughts. "Marcus! How's your mother? And how are you holding up, honey?"

The question caught him off guard, not just because of its directness, but because it reminded him that people still cared. Even here, in the quiet corners of his neighborhood, connection had always been waiting for him. It was humbling and heartwarming all at once.

On the walk home, his mind buzzed with ideas. Maybe he could start small—a conversation here, a coffee date there. Maybe he could join a support group, or even start one himself. The thought was both exhilarating and unnerving, his heartbeat quickening at the prospect of stepping out from behind his carefully constructed walls.

Healing, Marcus realized, was never meant to be a solo journey. It wasn't just about confronting pain—it was about finding the people who could help you carry the load when it got too heavy to bear alone.

Why is it often so difficult for us to seek out connections when we need them most?

The answer, Marcus knew, lay in fear—fear of judgment, fear of rejection, fear of being seen in all our messy, imperfect humanity. But as he thought about Mrs. Johnson's genuine concern and the warmth of a community he had taken for granted, he felt a flicker of hope. Maybe, just maybe, he didn't have to face this battle alone.

Who Said You Have to Go It Alone?

Let's cut to the chase: healing from maternal wounds isn't a one-man show. It's about time we debunk the myth of the lone wolf overcoming his struggles solo. The truth is, **community is essential**. Think about it; when you're dealing with the emotional aftermath of a strained or broken maternal relationship, the last thing you need is isolation adding to that burden. This chapter dives into why finding your tribe can be a game-changer in your healing journey.

The power of community can't be overstated. When you connect with others who've walked similar paths, there's an instant sense of 'I get you.' It's like finding out you're not the only one who hates pineapple on pizza – suddenly, you're not alone! This shared understanding creates a safe space where healing begins. Here, you can drop the mask and get real about your feelings, something that's hard to do in everyday scenarios where people might not grasp the depth of your experiences.

So, how do you start building these connections? First, acknowledge that **seeking help and community is a sign of strength**, not weakness. It's about being smart enough to know that together, we can rise stronger. Look for support groups, both online and offline, dedicated to men dealing with family issues or emotional healing. These groups provide a platform to share stories and strategies that can be enlightening and affirming.

Next up, let's talk about being proactive in these spaces. Don't just show up; engage genuinely .Be present. Share your journey and listen actively to others. This reciprocal exchange fosters deeper relationships and builds a network that goes beyond surface-level interactions. Remember, this isn't about finding folks who will simply nod along but those who will challenge you constructively and support your growth.

Building this supportive network also means stepping out of your comfort zone at times. It involves being open to new perspectives and perhaps adjusting long-held beliefs about masculinity and vulnerability. Yes, it's okay for men to express emotions and seek support! In fact, it's healthy and healing.

Here's where things get even more interesting: as you form these connections, they begin to act as both mirror and window. They mirror back your own experiences and emotions, helping you process them more effectively. Simultaneously, they offer a window into different coping strategies and healing methods that might work for you too.

Lastly, nurture these relationships like they're gold because, frankly, they are! They provide encouragement on tough days and celebrate with you on good ones. They remind you that every step forward is a victory worth acknowledging.

Wrapping It Up: Finding Strength in Numbers

Let's bring this all home: healing from maternal wounds isn't a solo expedition through uncharted territory—it's a team sport. Finding your tribe isn't just a nice-to-have; it's a necessity. It's about replacing isolation with connection, silence with shared stories, and fear with collective courage.

But let's add another layer to this conversation. Building a tribe isn't just about receiving support—it's also about giving it. When you step into a community, you bring your own unique experiences, insights, and energy to the table. You're not just taking; you're contributing to the shared strength of the group. This mutual exchange creates something larger than the sum of its parts, a bond that reinforces healing for everyone involved.

And here's the kicker: leaning on others doesn't make you weak. In fact, it takes guts. It takes courage to admit you need help, to open up about your pain, and to let others see you as you are—scars, flaws, and all. But that's also where the magic happens. Vulnerability breeds connection, and connection fosters resilience.

Additional Food for Thought

- **Community as Accountability:** Surrounding yourself with supportive people not only helps you heal but also keeps you accountable. Your tribe can call you out (lovingly) when you retreat into old patterns and cheer you on as you step into new ones.

- **A New Definition of Strength:** It's time to redefine what it means to be strong. Strength isn't about toughing it out alone; it's about knowing when to lean on others. True resilience is built through relationships, not isolation.
- **Different Tribes for Different Needs:** Don't limit yourself to one community. You might find solace in a group of men tackling similar maternal wounds, but don't forget other sources of connection—mentors, close friends, or even family members who understand your journey. Each "tribe" adds a unique layer of support.

Healing isn't linear, and it isn't always pretty. But with a tribe beside you, the peaks feel higher, and the valleys feel less lonely. So, when the path gets rough—and it will—you'll have people to lean on, laugh with, and grow alongside.

Bottom Line

You don't have to face this alone. Healing maternal wounds isn't about proving how tough you are; it's about building a life that feels whole and fulfilling. And the good news? Your tribe is out there, ready and waiting to walk this path with you.

So take that first step. Start looking for your people, reach out, and show up. Healing is a journey, but together, it becomes a journey worth taking.

Acknowledge the Importance of Community in the Healing Journey

Healing is often visualized as a personal, deeply internal process. It's true, but that's only half the picture. When it comes to healing from maternal wounds, the value of a supportive community cannot be overstated. Imagine trying to lift a heavy weight all by yourself; now, picture having a team with you, each ready to help hoist that weight up. That's what a community does when you're healing—it helps lift the burdens that are too heavy to bear alone.

Research shows that individuals who engage with supportive groups experience significant improvements in their psychological well-being. This is particularly crucial for those dealing with emotional scars like maternal wounds, where feelings of isolation can be overwhelming. A community provides not just emotional support but also practical advice and shared experiences that are invaluable during recovery.

Let's talk about vulnerability for a minute. Opening up about personal wounds can feel like walking into a storm without an umbrella—intimidating and exposing. However, finding your tribe means discovering a space where your vulnerabilities are not liabilities but bridges to deeper connections with others who understand and empathize.

Community is not just about receiving support; it's also about giving it. When you contribute to the healing of others, you find purpose and reinforcement in your own journey, creating a positive feedback loop of encouragement and understanding.

Community is essential in the healing journey as it provides both support and an opportunity for personal contribution, enhancing overall recovery.

Explore Ways to Connect with Others Who Have Similar Experiences

How do you find people who get it? Who understand the deep-seated issues tied to maternal wounds without needing an elaborate explanation? It starts by being proactive in seeking out groups and spaces where conversations about emotional health are encouraged.

Start by looking into local support groups specifically geared towards men dealing with family-related emotional issues. These groups provide a platform for sharing experiences and learning from others who face similar challenges. Engaging with such groups can significantly reduce feelings of isolation.

Online forums and social media platforms offer another avenue to connect. Many online communities are dedicated to specific healing journeys—be they related to parental relationships, mental health struggles, or personal development. These spaces allow for anonymity and accessibility, which can be comforting for those who are initially hesitant to share their stories in more public or face-to-face settings.

Consider attending workshops and seminars focused on emotional healing and personal growth. These events not only provide valuable information but also give you the chance to meet others who are on similar paths. It's like finding teammates who are playing the same sport on different fields—there's an inherent understanding and camaraderie that forms almost instantly.

Finding your tribe involves stepping out of your comfort zone and into environments where your experiences and feelings are validated by others' similar stories.

Build a Supportive Network to Share Insights and Encouragement

Once connections are made, how do you nurture these relationships into a robust network? It begins with regular interactions—sharing successes as well as setbacks. This consistent communication builds trust and deepens relationships over time, transforming them from mere acquaintances into pivotal support systems.

Create or join peer mentoring programs within these communities. Such initiatives encourage mutual growth through shared knowledge and experiences. It's akin to having both a coach and a cheerleader by your side—someone who pushes you towards your goals while also celebrating your victories, no matter how small.

Don't underestimate the power of informal gatherings or meet-ups either. Sometimes, a casual environment is exactly what's needed for people to open up and share more freely without the pressures that formal settings can impose.

Remember, the strength of your network lies not just in numbers but in the quality of connections—the kind that fosters genuine interaction and heartfelt support.

To build lasting relationships within your community,

actively participate in both giving and receiving advice, sharing experiences, and showing up for each other consistently.

By acknowledging the importance of community in our healing journeys, actively seeking connections with those who share similar experiences, and building supportive networks for ongoing encouragement, we empower ourselves toward profound personal growth and healing.

Healing from maternal wounds isn't a solo gig—it's a full-blown ensemble act. Acknowledging the importance of community in this healing journey isn't just about having people around; it's about having the **right** people around. Those who get the highs and lows, the ugly cries, and the breakthrough laughs. It's about building a circle that stands by you, not just when you're shining, but especially when you're not.

Finding your tribe is like finding your rhythm in the chaos of recovery. It's about connecting with others who nod knowingly when you share your story because they've been there too. It's not just sharing space, but sharing struggles and victories. This connection fosters a sense of belonging that many have missed in their initial upbringing.

Building a supportive network is essentially equipping

yourself with your own personal cheerleading squad—but better. They're there to provide insights, throw down a challenge when needed, and offer encouragement that sticks. This network becomes your sounding board and your reality check, vital for keeping both feet on the ground while reaching for healing.

Let's keep it real; confronting emotional scars can feel like reopening old wounds at times. But with a tribe that stands ready to empower and empathize, these moments become opportunities for growth rather than retreat. The shared experiences within these communities help dilute the loneliness that often accompanies healing from deep-rooted issues.

Remember, every step taken towards connecting with others on similar paths is a step away from isolation and a step closer to holistic health. Mind, body, and spirit are all in this dance together—none should be left behind.

So as you move forward, keep this in mind: **Your tribe is out there**. Finding them might require stepping out of comfort zones or breaking old patterns. But once found, they enrich your journey with layers of support and understanding that solo endeavors simply cannot match.

Embrace this communal aspect of healing with open arms

and an open heart—it's not just beneficial, it's essential. And hey, let's be real; walking this path with others makes the journey not just bearable but also beautifully transformative.

Chapter 4: The Holistic Healing Handbook

The first rays of morning light crept through the blinds of Marcus's kitchen, painting golden stripes across the worn wooden table. Marcus sat there, his broad hands wrapped around a mug of steaming tea. The faint scent of chamomile rose with the steam, swirling lazily in the air as if to match his scattered thoughts. Outside the window, the world was waking up—birds chirped, a car rumbled to life down the street, and the soft hum of distant voices hinted at a new day.

But Marcus wasn't quite ready to join the world outside. His mind wandered back to the relentless echoes of his past: his father's sharp words, the heavy weight of expectations that felt more like shackles than guidance. These weren't just memories—they were ghosts, lingering in the corners of his mind, ready to pounce in moments of silence.

He sighed, his shoulders rising and falling under the weight of it all. The tea was warm in his hands, grounding him as he stared out the window at the streaks of orange and pink lighting up the sky. He wasn't the type to wallow—Marcus was a doer, the kind of guy who fixed things. Yet fixing himself felt like the most complicated project of all.

The chirping of birds jolted him back to the present. Marcus shook his head as if to physically banish the thoughts clinging to him. He had been reading about holistic approaches to healing—things like setting boundaries, nourishing his body, and fostering mindfulness. Maybe it was time to stop overthinking and start doing.

As he sipped his tea, a memory surfaced: the time he'd said yes to helping a neighbor build a deck, even though his back was killing him from work the day before. He'd ignored his own needs then, just like he always did. That had to change. Marcus was beginning to understand that self-care wasn't selfish—it was necessary.

His phone buzzed, pulling his attention to the screen. A message from an old friend flashed across it: **"Hey, can you help with the food drive this weekend?"**

Marcus's thumb hovered over the keyboard, old instincts urging him to type "yes" without hesitation. But then he paused, hearing a new voice inside—the one he was working hard to cultivate. "I need some time," he typed instead. The words felt strange, like trying on a jacket that didn't quite fit, but they also felt... right. A quiet triumph stirred in his chest.

The rest of the morning unfolded like a slow, deliberate symphony. Marcus repotted an overgrown plant sitting by the window. As he gently loosened the tangled roots and placed them in fresh soil, he couldn't help but feel a kinship with the plant. Growth wasn't easy—it required letting go of what no longer served and embracing something new, even when it felt uncomfortable.

By noon, the kitchen was filled with the savory aroma of grilled chicken and sautéed greens. Marcus sat at the table, savoring the simple meal and reflecting on the parallels between nourishing his body and his soul. He realized that healing wasn't a one-dimensional process. It required layers of care: physical, emotional, and mental.

After lunch, Marcus leaned back in his chair, staring at the now-empty plate. He felt a rare sense of peace settle over him. This wasn't about grand, sweeping changes—it was about small, deliberate acts that added up over time. For the first time in weeks, he felt grounded.

As he cleared the table and washed the dishes, Marcus found himself smiling. His journey toward healing wasn't about denying his past or pretending he wasn't still carrying scars. It was about building resilience through intentional actions. He wasn't just surviving anymore—he was starting to thrive.

Doesn't Marcus's story remind us of the delicate balance every man must learn to strike? Strength isn't about stoicism; it's about knowing when to let go, when to grow, and when to ask for help. Healing isn't a quick fix—it's a daily practice, a commitment to nurturing yourself just as much as you nurture the world around you. And in those small, steady steps, transformation begins.

Unpacking the Toolbox: A Guide to Holistic Healing

Healing from maternal wounds is not a straightforward journey; it is layered, deeply personal, and requires a multifaceted approach. For many men, these wounds manifest as emotional scars that influence their interactions and personal growth throughout life. Recognizing the complexity of these issues, this chapter delves into an integrated healing approach that combines various methodologies to address the underlying trauma, build resilience, and foster genuine connections.

The emotional burden of unresolved maternal wounds can be staggering. It often hampers one's ability to establish trust, form healthy relationships, or maintain a positive self-image. **Integrating various healing approaches** provides a robust framework for tackling these deep-seated issues. This isn't about choosing one method over another but about creating a blend that addresses emotional, psychological, and spiritual needs.

To embark on this journey of comprehensive recovery, it's crucial to first understand the nature of your wounds. This involves introspection and possibly revisiting painful memories to identify specific incidents or patterns that have left a lasting impact. The process is challenging but necessary to lay a clear foundation for healing.

Developing personal resilience is another critical aspect discussed in this chapter. Resilience doesn't mean you won't feel pain or face setbacks; rather, it's about equipping yourself with tools like self-care practices and boundary setting to navigate through adversity without losing your sense of self. Establishing boundaries is particularly vital as it helps protect your emotional space from being compromised by past triggers or current pressures.

Creating a **personalized healing plan** is where theory meets practice. This plan isn't just a checklist; it's a dynamic strategy tailored to individual experiences and goals. It involves selecting therapeutic approaches that resonate with you—be it conventional therapy, support groups, creative expression, or spiritual practices—and integrating them into a cohesive routine that champions steady healing.

Crafting Your Healing Blueprint: Building Your Game Plan

Let's be honest—creating a healing plan isn't the sexiest thing on the to-do list. But this isn't about checking boxes; it's about building a strategy that actually works for you. Think of it as designing a playbook for the most important game of your life: becoming the strongest, most balanced version of yourself. And just like any winning strategy, this plan isn't set in stone—it's adaptable, personal, and rooted in what resonates with *you*.

You're not here to fix yourself overnight. You're here to take deliberate, meaningful steps toward growth. So, let's get down to business:

Step 1: Spot the Emotional Bruises

Before you can tackle the enemy, you've got to know where they're hiding. Take some time to reflect on the emotional scars you're carrying. Are they showing up in your relationships? Your confidence? Your ability to trust? Think about how these wounds are shaping the way you interact with the world. Knowing what you're up against is your first move toward healing

Step 2: Scout Your Options

Healing isn't one-size-fits-all, so this is your chance to explore what feels right for you. From psychotherapy and support groups to mindfulness practices and creative outlets, there's a world of tools at your disposal. Look into them with an open mind—what catches your attention? What feels doable? This is about finding the approaches that *fit* you, not forcing yourself into a mold.

Step 3: Go All-In on Holistic Healing

You're not just a brain, or just a body, or just a heart—you're a whole person, and your healing plan should reflect that. Pair mental and emotional work with physical and spiritual care. Maybe that's therapy and journaling paired with exercise and meditation. Maybe it's something entirely unique to you. The point is to cover all the bases so you can rebuild from the ground up.

Step 4: Set Goals Like a Boss

Healing isn't just about feeling better—it's about knowing where you're going. Take the time to define what "healing" means to you. Is it better relationships? Greater self-confidence? Less baggage? Use SMART goals (specific, measurable, achievable, relevant, and time-bound) to create a clear vision for your progress.

Step 5: Break it Down Like a Playlist

Big goals can feel overwhelming, so chop them into bite-sized pieces. If your goal is to "improve communication," start with smaller steps like learning active listening techniques or practicing expressing your needs. Every small win adds up, building momentum that keeps you moving forward.

Step 6: Schedule Like You Mean It

You're busy—we get it. But healing can't happen on the back burner. Carve out time for your practices, whether it's a therapy session, a mindfulness exercise, or a 15-minute journal entry. Think of it as non-negotiable "you time." Treat it like an appointment you wouldn't dare miss.

Step 7: Track the Wins (and the Setbacks)

Keep a journal to document your journey. Write about what's working, what's not, and how you're feeling along the way. This isn't just about progress—it's about processing. Seeing how far you've come (even if it's messy) can be a powerful motivator.

Step 8: Pivot When Needed

Life throws curveballs, and your healing plan should be flexible enough to handle them. Maybe a particular strategy doesn't feel right anymore—that's okay. Adjust as you learn more about what helps you thrive. Healing is about growth, and growth means evolving.

Step 9: Call in the Reinforcements

There's no shame in asking for help. Seek out professionals, mentors, or friends who can support you along the way. A therapist, a men's group, or even a close buddy who gets it can make a world of difference. Healing isn't a solo act—it's a team effort.

Step 10: Celebrate the Hell Out of Yourself

You did the work. You faced the pain. You showed up, day after day, and that's worth celebrating. Whether it's a small win (like setting a boundary) or a big milestone (like feeling at peace with a tough memory), take the time to acknowledge your victories. Treat yourself, share the moment, or just sit back and let it sink in—you're making progress.

The Final Word

Your healing plan isn't about perfection—it's about persistence. It's about showing up for yourself in ways that matter. Each step, no matter how small, is a testament to your strength and commitment to growth. And as you build this blueprint, remember: it's not just about recovering from the past—it's about creating the future you deserve. Let's get to work.

Integrating Various Healing Approaches for Comprehensive Recovery

When we talk about healing, especially from deep-seated wounds like those from maternal relationships, it's akin to fixing a complex engine. Each part of the engine plays a crucial role, and if one part fails, it affects the whole system. Similarly, using a variety of healing methods—be it therapy, self-help groups, or personal reflection—ensures we address all aspects of our well-being.

Therapy might help you unravel the knots of your past, while meditation could serve as your daily tool to maintain mental peace. Adding physical exercise can boost your overall energy levels and improve mood. It's not just about choosing one approach; it's about creating a blend that suits your unique needs.

Imagine you're cooking a stew. You wouldn't just throw in a single spice and call it a day. Healing is much the same; it requires different 'ingredients' or approaches to truly nourish your mind and soul. Some days you might need more of one thing than another, and that's perfectly okay.

Self-help books often provide strategies that resonate differently with everyone. They can offer insights that click something into place or introduce new coping mechanisms that hadn't been considered before. It's about finding what speaks to you personally.

Engaging in community activities or support groups can also play an integral role. Connecting with others who share similar experiences can validate your feelings and foster a sense of belonging.

Combining various healing approaches creates a robust framework for comprehensive recovery from emotional wounds.

Develop Personal Resilience Through Self-Care and Boundary Setting

One undeniable truth in the journey of healing is the power of self-care and establishing boundaries. Just as a castle has its walls to protect those within from harm, setting boundaries protects your mental space from negative influences.

Self-care is not just about pampering yourself but ensuring you're in a good place mentally and physically. It includes activities like getting enough sleep, eating nutritious foods, and engaging in hobbies that bring you joy. Think of it as maintaining your car so it doesn't break down—you're doing regular checks and balances on yourself.

Boundaries are essential; they are the rules we set around our time, energy, and interactions with others. When these are clearly defined and respected, stress levels often decrease, leading to improved mental health.

Consider how a tree uses its roots for stability and nourishment but also has the bark as a protective barrier. In human relationships, boundaries act like this bark—protecting us from external harm while allowing us to form healthy connections.

Now, imagine having a toolbox where each tool has its specific purpose in fixing a particular problem—the same goes for self-care practices and boundary-setting techniques in managing life's challenges.

But how do you know which tools to use and when? This is where personal intuition and advice from trusted sources come into play. You learn which practices best suit your personal needs through trial and experience.

What would happen if you truly honored your needs and set boundaries without guilt?

Create A Personalized Healing Plan That Addresses Emotional Scars

Holistic Healing Model

The Holistic Healing Model (HHM) offers an integrated approach to tackling the multifaceted nature of emotional scars left by maternal wounds. This model is not just about addressing one aspect of health but ensuring all areas are considered for balanced healing.

Emotional Awareness

At the core of HHM lies Emotional Awareness—this involves recognizing and processing emotions linked to past traumas. Techniques such as journaling or therapy sessions help unearth these emotions so they can be faced head-on rather than letting them fester unacknowledged.

Physical Health

Physical Health focuses on activities promoting bodily wellness like regular exercise or proper nutrition. There's substantial evidence showing how physical health impacts emotional wellbeing—improving one often leads to improvements in the other.

Social Connectivity

Then there's Social Connectivity which emphasizes building supportive networks through friendships, support groups, or professional help like therapists. We heal better together than isolated; sharing experiences can lighten our emotional loads significantly.

Mental Resilience

Finally, Mental Resilience encapsulates strategies for building psychological strength through practices such as mindfulness or adopting positive thinking patterns. It's about developing tools to handle stress better when it inevitably comes knocking at your door.

Each component interacts with others; improving Emotional Awareness might reduce social anxieties enhancing Social Connectivity which in turn may bolster Mental Resilience by reducing feelings of loneliness.

By integrating various healing approaches—self-care routines, boundary-setting practices, and designing personalized healing plans—a holistic recovery becomes more than achievable; it becomes transformative for men grappling with maternal wounds.

As we wrap up this chapter, let's hold onto the golden nugget: integrating various healing approaches isn't just a good strategy; it's a game-changer for anyone serious about conquering their emotional scars. It's like having the best tools in your toolkit when you're ready to tackle a major home improvement project—except the home is your soul, and the improvements are for your well-being.

Remember, resilience isn't born overnight. It's cultivated by consistent self-care and setting those boundaries that say, "Hey, I matter too." Think of it as building muscle at the gym—every day you lift those emotional weights, you get stronger. And let's face it, who doesn't feel a bit of pride when they see their progress? So, flex those resilience muscles with pride!

Now, crafting your personalized healing plan is akin to drawing up a personal treasure map. Each part of the map guides you through the rough terrains of the past hurts towards the treasure of emotional freedom. Yes, it requires effort, and yes, there will be days when it feels like two steps forward and one step back. But remember, even on those tough days, you're still making progress.

Embrace this journey with an open heart and mind. The integration of mind, body, and spirit within your healing process isn't just holistic mumbo-jumbo; it's about creating harmony within yourself. When these elements align, not only do you heal but you also unlock new realms of potential within yourself—potentials for happiness, peace, and fulfilling relationships.

So go ahead! Take what you've learned here and start applying it. Be bold in your self-care; be strategic in setting your boundaries; be thoughtful as you craft your healing plan. Remember that every step forward is a step towards not just healing but becoming the version of yourself you aspire to be.

Let this chapter serve as a springboard into deeper waters where you're not just surviving but thriving. Because at the end of the day, isn't that what we all want? To thrive in a life that feels authentically ours? Here's to that journey—may it be as enlightening as it is liberating!

Chapter 5: The Mirror of Self-Awareness

Marcus walked through the crisp autumn air of the city park, his hands buried deep in the pockets of his worn leather jacket. The leaves, a riot of reds and golds, crunched satisfyingly underfoot, their decay a stark reminder of nature's cycles. His mind was elsewhere though, tangled in thoughts that traced back to his childhood, to his mother's stern voice and cold silences.

He paused by the park's small pond, watching as a couple of ducks glided serenely across the water. The scene was peaceful, almost painfully so. Marcus felt a familiar tightening in his chest—the lingering ache of maternal wounds that had shaped so much of who he was; an architect not just of buildings but of walls around his own heart.

As he stood there, memories surfaced unbidden: missed birthdays, harsh words spoken too freely, affection withheld at crucial moments. These fragments from the past often visited him during such solitary moments, each memory pointing to why trust felt like a bridge too frail to tread upon.

Marcus shook his head slightly as if to dispel the gathering shadows of his thoughts and started walking again. His steps took him along a path lined with benches where an old man sat feeding pigeons. The sight brought a wry smile to Marcus's lips; even these birds were sustained by a hand gentler than those he had known.

The park was nearing its end and so was this walk—a daily practice in mindfulness that Marcus clung to as one might cling to a lifeline. It grounded him, gave him perspective and sometimes, on good days, it loosened the tight knots of feelings enough for him to breathe easier.

Yet today, questions lingered heavy in the air like the last notes of a song long ended—could understanding these wounds ever lead him truly beyond them? Could recognizing their impact really untangle the complex emotions they bred?

As he exited the park and merged with the flow of city life around him—each person swathed in their own stories—Marcus knew this journey toward healing wasn't linear or predictable. But perhaps today's reflections brought him closer to finding peace amid chaos; maybe today's insights were steps towards mending bridges long thought beyond repair.

And isn't it true that every journey begins with understanding where you stand?

Unveiling the Hidden Threads: How Your Mother's Influence Shapes You

Self-awareness isn't just a buzzword—it's a crucial tool for anyone looking to mend the emotional scars left by a maternal wound. For many men, understanding how these deep-seated issues influence their thoughts and behaviors can be both enlightening and transformative. It's about peeling back the layers of your emotional onion without shedding too many tears—unless you need to, of course!

In this journey towards self-discovery, it's vital to recognize that our mothers often lay the first bricks of our emotional foundations. These interactions can shape our views on trust, love, and security. For those who have experienced less-than-ideal maternal relationships, this influence can manifest in unexpected ways—perhaps in your relentless perfectionism or your hesitancy in forming close relationships. By **gaining insights** into these patterns, you're not just reading an old diary; you're decoding the blueprint of your emotional construct.

Now, don't get it twisted; this isn't about playing the blame game. It's about gaining clarity. Practicing **mindfulness** is like having a high-definition mirror showing what's inside you. It allows you to observe your mental and emotional processes without judgment. This practice isn't just about sitting quietly—it's about engaging actively with your thoughts and feelings, understanding them more deeply as they occur.

Starting the process of **untangling your emotional complexities** might sound as daunting as solving a Rubik's cube blindfolded. But here's the kicker: you are the only one who can truly navigate through this intricate maze. Every man has his own unique set of experiences that colors his view of the world. Recognizing and accepting these colors can profoundly change how you relate to others—and more importantly, how you relate to yourself.

Let's consider resilience—not just a fancy word we hear thrown around at work or on tiktok but as a lived experience. Overcoming challenges related to maternal wounds requires resilience not just in big, life-changing decisions, but in everyday reactions and choices. This chapter arms you with the tools not only to survive but thrive by transforming wounds into wisdom.

The connection between mind, body, and spirit is undeniable in this healing process. When one is out of sync, the whole system feels it! Engaging in holistic practices that nurture each aspect can lead to more profound insights and more sustainable healing. This isn't just about feeling better—it's about being better.

As we wrap up this exploration into self-awareness, remember this: knowledge is power—power to change, grow, and heal. Armed with this power, stepping out from under the long shadow cast by maternal wounds becomes not just possible but inevitable.

So let's get moving! It's time to turn those insights into action and those actions into a path toward genuine emotional freedom.

Understanding the Impact of Maternal Wounds on Thoughts and Behaviors

Maternal wounds often lurk beneath the surface of our daily interactions and decisions, subtly influencing our lives in ways we may not fully recognize. These wounds, formed from the fractures in early nurturing relationships, particularly with mothers, can manifest as patterns in our thoughts and behaviors. For instance, a man who grew up with a critical mother might find himself overly critical or excessively defensive in his personal relationships.

To explore this further, consider the analogy of a garden. If the soil is poor and neglected, even the most resilient seeds struggle to flourish. Similarly, when maternal nurturing is lacking, it can stunt emotional growth, making it difficult for positive behaviors and healthy thought patterns to take root.

Research has consistently shown that early maternal relationships shape our adult attachment styles. Those with secure attachments tend to have healthier relationships and more stable self-images compared to those with insecure attachments who might struggle with self-worth and trust issues. This insight is crucial because it highlights how deeply maternal wounds can influence one's life trajectory.

In real terms, this means everyday interactions can be a minefield. A man might misinterpret constructive criticism at work as personal attacks, mirroring the unfounded critiques he received from his mother during childhood. This misinterpretation stems not from the present reality but from a deep-seated memory imprinted by past wounds.

Understanding how maternal wounds affect us can empower us to make conscious changes in our thoughts and behaviors.

The Role of Mindfulness in Enhancing Self-Understanding

Mindfulness is like a flashlight in the darkness of our unconscious patterns; it illuminates insights that are often obscured by the hustle of daily life. By practicing mindfulness, one learns to observe their thoughts and feelings without judgment, which is essential for those healing from maternal wounds.

Consider mindfulness practice as tuning an instrument before a performance; it's about fine-tuning your mind's reactions to emotions and thoughts stirred up by past experiences. This tuning allows you to respond rather than react—creating music from what was once noise.

Mindfulness has been supported by numerous studies indicating its benefits in reducing stress, anxiety, and depression—all common symptoms experienced by individuals dealing with unresolved emotional issues from childhood. It encourages a state of awareness that helps individuals recognize patterns they have unconsciously enacted due to maternal influences.

By adopting mindfulness techniques such as meditation or mindful breathing, you gain a clearer understanding of how your past affects your present. This clarity doesn't come all at once but develops over time as you regularly engage in these practices.

Through mindfulness, you can start noticing when your reactions are disproportionate to the situation at hand—perhaps triggered by old wounds rather than current events. This awareness is the first step towards changing these reactions.

As you become more practiced in mindfulness, you'll likely find moments of peace previously clouded by unaddressed emotions related to your maternal relationship. It's about gaining freedom through understanding oneself better.

Could recognizing these moments be the key to unlocking your true potential?

Beginning to Untangle Emotional Complexities

Starting the process of untangling emotional complexities requires an honest look at oneself—an examination that goes beyond surface-level understanding. It involves delving into the nuances of your emotions and understanding where they stem from.

Imagine trying to detangle a heavily knotted necklace; patience and gentle probing are required to avoid breaking it altogether. Similarly, addressing deep-seated emotional wounds necessitates a careful approach that respects the complexity of human emotions.

One effective method for beginning this process is journaling. Writing down thoughts and feelings can act as a mirror reflecting back your emotional state over time. This reflection can reveal patterns or triggers linked to maternal wounds that might not be evident in day-to-day living.

Another approach involves therapy or counseling—a professional setting where one can explore their emotions safely under guidance. Therapists specialize in helping individuals recognize sources of their distress and developing strategies for addressing them healthily and constructively.

As these tangled emotions begin to unravel through consistent effort—whether via self-help strategies like journaling or professional guidance—you gain insights that are crucial for healing. Over time, this leads to improved emotional resilience and healthier relationships with others and oneself.

Each step taken towards understanding how maternal wounds affect us, practicing mindfulness for better self-awareness, and untangling complex emotions leads

us closer to true healing and personal growth.

These learning objectives guide us through recognizing past influences on present realities, embracing techniques for greater self-awareness, and actively working on emotional complexities for holistic well-being.

Understanding the impact of maternal wounds on our thoughts and behaviors is more than just a trip down memory lane; it's a vital step in reclaiming your life. By now, you've likely realized that these wounds don't just fade with time—they need intentional action. **Gaining insights** into how these deep-seated issues shape your world is like flipping on a light switch in a dark room. Suddenly, things start to make sense, and what once seemed like random patterns in your behavior begin to reveal their origins.

Practicing mindfulness isn't just about sitting quietly; it's about becoming the boss of your inner landscape. It's like having a mental broom to sweep away the clutter, allowing you to face your challenges head-on. When you enhance self-understanding through mindfulness, you're not just going through the motions; you're engaging in a form of mental strength training. This isn't about getting rid of emotions but managing them with a finesse that would make even the most stoic philosophers give you a nod of respect.

Now, let's talk about untangling emotional complexities—this isn't for the faint-hearted. But hey, who said you weren't up for a challenge? Starting this process is akin to unraveling a tightly wound knot. It takes patience, persistence, and sometimes just the stubbornness to not give up. Each thread pulled can reveal more about your motivations, fears, and desires. And yes, while this can feel daunting at times, remember—every step forward is a step towards a more authentic connection with yourself and others.

As we wrap up this chapter, remember that self-awareness is not just about introspection; it's an active, ongoing journey. It requires courage to look at the man in the mirror and ask the tough questions. But believe me when I say—the growth that comes from this journey is worth every bit of effort.

So keep pushing forward, keep unraveling those knots, and most importantly, keep shining that light on the corners of your mind that need it most. Your future self will thank you for it. And when times get tough? Remember this: You have the strength to face whatever comes your way—and then some.

Here's to moving forward with resilience and determination! Embrace this journey not just with hope but with a certainty that you are capable of healing and thriving beyond your wounds.

In the dim, gray light of early morning, Marcus sat on the edge of his bed, elbows resting on his knees, his hands clasped tightly together. The air was thick with the kind of silence that amplifies everything—the groan of pipes, the hum of the refrigerator, the muffled honk of a car in the distance. His thoughts, heavy and tangled, pulled him back to the same place they always did: his mother.

Their relationship was like a thorn bush—complex, tangled, and full of sharp edges. Some memories were tender, like the time she stayed up with him when he was sick. Others were cutting, like her sharp words on the day he didn't make the varsity basketball team. These moments wove a tapestry of unresolved feelings that he carried like a weight on his shoulders.

But today felt different. Today, Marcus decided, would be the day he started cutting through the thorns to find some space to breathe.

He stood and shuffled to the kitchen, the floor cool beneath his bare feet. The familiar hiss and clank of the kettle being filled with water brought him back to the present. He struck a match, lit the stove, and watched the flame dance to life beneath the kettle. There was something oddly reassuring about the ritual—simple, steady, and grounding.

As the water heated, Marcus leaned against the counter, letting last night's therapy session replay in his mind. His therapist had leaned forward, her voice soft but insistent: "Self-compassion isn't a luxury, Marcus. It's a necessity. You can't heal without it."

He had scoffed at first, the way men often do when told to "be kind to yourself." It sounded fluffy, weak. But as she explained it, something clicked. "Think about how quick you are to forgive your friends, to cut them some slack. Why not give yourself the same grace?"

The kettle whistled, breaking his train of thought. Marcus poured the boiling water over a tea bag, watching as the rich amber color spread through the cup. The steam curled upward, and for a moment, he just stood there, holding the mug in both hands, letting its warmth seep into his palms.

This wasn't just tea today—it was a step, a deliberate act of choosing himself. He carried the mug to his favorite armchair, the one by the window, and sank into its familiar cushions.

Outside, the city was waking up. The orange hues of dawn stretched across the sky, painting a picture of renewal.

Marcus stared out at the skyline, his thoughts now quieter, more reflective. He took a slow sip of tea, letting its warmth fill him, not just physically but emotionally, too.

As he sat there, he thought about forgiveness—not just for his mother but for himself. For the times he'd lashed out in anger when he really felt hurt. For the moments he'd tried to be invincible when he should have allowed himself to break. Forgiveness, he realized, wasn't about rewriting the past—it was about choosing peace in the present.

His phone buzzed on the coffee table, its screen lighting up with a notification. An email? A group chat message? He didn't check. Not yet. Instead, he closed his eyes, took a deep breath, and let it go. This moment was his, and he wasn't going to let it slip away.

How might life shift if we treated ourselves with the same kindness we so freely offer to others? Marcus let the question linger, not just in his mind but in his heart.

The answer, he suspected, wasn't about a single revelation or grand gesture. It was about small, deliberate acts of self-compassion. Choosing to sit with his tea. Choosing to forgive himself for not always getting it right. Choosing to show up for himself, thorns and all.

This wasn't the end of his journey—not by a long shot. But for the first time, it felt like he had found a map. And maybe, just maybe, that was enough for today.

Who Said Being Kind to Yourself Was Easy?

Let's get one thing straight: **self-compassion isn't just about giving yourself a break or indulging in extra dessert.** It's a crucial, healing tool, especially when you're dealing with the kind of deep-seated emotional scars that come from maternal wounds. For many men, the journey towards understanding and healing these wounds involves confronting pain they've carried since childhood—pain that can shape how they interact with the world and themselves.

In this exploration, we're diving into why kindness to oneself is not just beneficial but essential. It's about transforming the inner critic—that often harsh internal voice—into a supportive ally. Yes, that relentless critic can become your biggest cheerleader. Imagine transforming those self-critical thoughts into affirmations that not only soothe but empower.

Embracing self-kindness means acknowledging that healing isn't a linear process and that it's okay to have moments of vulnerability. Vulnerability isn't a sign of weakness; it's a badge of courage. It shows you're in the arena, fighting the good fight to heal and grow. Recognizing and accepting where you are in this process is pivotal because it aligns with the reality of your experiences rather than an unattainable ideal.

Now, let's talk about *employing self-compassion practices* to ease these wounds. This isn't about quick fixes but cultivating practices that foster long-term healing and resilience. Techniques like mindfulness meditation or simply taking moments to breathe deeply can significantly shift your emotional state. These practices help create a space between your feelings and reactions, providing room to choose how to respond to life's challenges more thoughtfully.

Moreover, self-compassion arms you with **resilience**. This resilience doesn't mean you won't feel pain or face setbacks; instead, it means you'll be better equipped to handle them. When you're kinder to yourself, you recognize that setbacks are not reflections of your worth but opportunities for growth and learning.

Resilience also fosters self-acceptance—another critical element on this journey. Self-acceptance invites you to embrace all parts of yourself—the good, the bad, and everything in between. It encourages a healthier internal dialogue that acknowledges accomplishments and gently learns from missteps without harsh judgment.

Laugh at the Chaos

It's also important to maintain a sense of humor about oneself and the healing journey. Let's be real: sometimes you have to laugh to keep from crying! A light-hearted approach can make heavy moments feel lighter and remind us not to take ourselves too seriously all the time.

Through this chapter's insights and strategies, embracing self-compassion becomes less of an abstract concept and more of a tangible practice that guides men through healing maternal wounds with grace and strength. By fostering kindness towards oneself, employing mindful self-compassion practices, and navigating emotional challenges with resilience and acceptance, healing becomes not just possible but probable.

So here's your takeaway: Be as generous with compassion for yourself as you would be for others—it's not just nice; it's necessary for healing. And remember, every step forward in this journey is a step towards not just surviving but thriving.

Embrace Kindness Towards Oneself as a Healing Tool

Kindness, often seen as a simple act directed towards others, is equally vital when turned inward. For men grappling with maternal wounds, this self-directed kindness isn't just a nice-to-have; it's a cornerstone of healing. When you treat yourself with the same compassion and understanding that you might offer to a good friend, you begin to mend the internalized hurt and rejection that such deep-seated wounds can cause.

Imagine your self-compassion as a soothing balm, gently applied to the raw areas of your spirit injured by maternal neglect or misunderstanding. Just as a physical wound requires clean bandages and ointments, your emotional injuries need tenderness and care. By nurturing yourself, you create an environment conducive to healing, rather than one that perpetuates pain.

Research underscores the transformative power of self-kindness. Studies in psychological science suggest that individuals who practice self-compassion tend to experience lower levels of depression and anxiety. They are not only kinder to themselves but also bounce back more readily from setbacks, viewing them not as insurmountable failures but as opportunities for growth and learning.

Yet, embracing this practice can be challenging, especially for those who've rarely received compassion themselves. It requires a deliberate shift in mindset—from harsh self-criticism to an encouraging inner voice. Think of it as reprogramming a computer; old, negative scripts are replaced with positive affirmations that assert your worth and potential.

Self-kindness is an essential tool for healing from maternal wounds.

Employ Self-Compassion Practices to Ease the Pain of Maternal Wounds

The journey toward healing from maternal wounds is deeply personal and can often be complex. Self-compassion practices serve as critical navigational tools in this process, helping to alleviate the emotional burden these wounds carry. Engaging in these practices isn't about ignoring the pain but about addressing it with gentleness and understanding.

Mindfulness is one such practice that stands out for its effectiveness. It involves staying present and fully experiencing what comes without judgment. When feelings of inadequacy or rejection surface—common emotions stemming from maternal wounds—mindfulness allows you to observe these feelings without becoming overwhelmed by them.

Consider how mindfulness works: It's like observing the waves in the ocean from the shore. You notice them rise and fall, their ebb and flow, but you remain safely on the beach—detached yet aware. This metaphor highlights how mindfulness helps manage emotional turbulence; you recognize your feelings without letting them pull you under.

Adding to mindfulness are specific exercises like **self-soothing techniques** which include deep breathing, meditation, or even engaging in activities that you find comforting or joyful. These practices reinforce the idea that you deserve care and comfort, directly countering any narratives of unworthiness inherited from parental relationships.

Writing letters to oneself can also be profoundly therapeutic in cultivating self-compassion. This exercise involves writing words of encouragement and understanding to oneself just as you would console a dear friend. This method reinforces internal support systems that maternal relationships may have failed to develop.

By integrating these practices into daily life, they gradually transform the internal landscape marked by scars into one where growth and self-acceptance flourish.

Could realizing your own worth through gentle self-dialogue be the key to unlocking deeper healing?

Navigate Emotional Challenges with Resilience and Self-Acceptance

Navigating emotional challenges with resilience involves more than just enduring; it's about thriving amidst adversity. For men healing from maternal wounds, this means not only surviving the day-to-day struggles but also emerging stronger and more self-aware from each challenge.

Resilience is built through a combination of self-awareness, acceptance, and proactive emotional management. When you become aware of your emotional triggers and acknowledge them without judgment, you set the stage for resilience. This awareness acts like a radar—alerting you when turbulent emotions approach so you can prepare rather than react impulsively.

Self-acceptance goes hand-in-hand with this awareness. It

involves embracing all aspects of yourself—the good and the challenging—and recognizing that your worth isn't tied to perfection or external approval (which might have been withheld in maternal relationships). Accepting oneself fully is akin to setting down a heavy load that you've been carrying unconsciously; it frees up energy for growth and joy.

Proactive emotional management is another key component. This could look like setting boundaries in relationships or pursuing therapy or counseling services which provide tools for dealing with complex emotions more effectively.

Together, these practices foster an environment where resilience can thrive—turning previous vulnerabilities into sources of strength.

By embracing kindness towards oneself, employing self-compassion practices regularly, and navigating emotional challenges with resilience and acceptance, individuals can transform their experiences with maternal wounds from sources of ongoing pain into opportunities for profound personal growth.

Embrace kindness towards oneself as a healing tool.

Let's be real: being kind to yourself can sometimes feel like a luxury you can't afford, especially when you're dealing with the heavy baggage of maternal wounds. But here's the kicker: self-kindness isn't just about feeling good—it's your secret weapon in the healing process. It's like applying a soothing balm to those raw emotional injuries. Remember, healing begins within, and how you talk to yourself can either lift you up or weigh you down. Choose to be your own biggest cheerleader, not your toughest critic.

Employ self-compassion practices to ease the pain of maternal wounds.

Now, onto the powerhouse practices of self-compassion—these aren't just fluffy concepts; they're practical tools that pack a punch. Whether it's mindfulness meditation, journaling your thoughts and feelings, or simply giving yourself permission to rest, these practices are about confronting those wounds with a gentleness that might feel foreign but is incredibly effective. Think of it this way: each act of self-compassion is a step towards not just managing pain but transforming it into your platform for growth.

Navigate emotional challenges with resilience and self-acceptance.

Navigating emotional challenges with resilience doesn't

mean you won't ever falter—hey, we're all human here! But it does mean recognizing that stumbling is part of the journey. Self-acceptance is giving yourself room to breathe, make mistakes, and still say, "I'm okay." It's about not letting your struggles define your worth but using them as stepping stones to rise stronger. And when you do rise? You'll not only surprise others but more importantly, you'll astonish yourself.

The Synergy of Mind, Body, and Spirit

Cultivating self-compassion is essentially about aligning the mind, body, and spirit in a harmonious symphony that fosters healing and growth. When these elements are in tune, navigating life's thorns becomes less about survival and more about thriving. By integrating practices that nurture all aspects of your being, you set the stage for profound transformations that extend beyond mere coping—ushering in a life marked by deeper connections and authentic joy.

So as we wrap up this chapter on nurturing self-compassion amidst the thorns of maternal wounds, remember: *the journey might be rugged*, but equipping yourself with kindness, compassion practices, and an attitude of resilience transforms the path ahead. It's time to turn those wounds into wisdom and pain into power. Keep stepping forward with heart and grit—because on this journey of healing, every step counts.

Chapter 7: The Art of Boundary Setting

In the gray light of dawn, Michael sat on the edge of his bed, a firm hand resting on his knee, feeling the cold bite of the morning through the cracked window. The air was heavy with the scent of rain and wet earth, a rawness that matched the restless energy inside him. His room was sparse, painted in the kind of muted blue that felt practical but unsentimental—no distractions, just the essentials. The calloused skin on his palms was proof of his life's work as a craftsman, shaping wood into furniture, solid and dependable. Today, however, his task was less about wood and more about words.

Michael's younger brother, James, had recently moved back to town. The guy had a habit of showing up unannounced, beers in hand, and while Michael enjoyed a good drink as much as the next man, he needed his space. His workshop was his fortress, his escape from the world—a place where he could think, work, and breathe. But James's surprise visits were throwing everything off balance, stirring up dust that Michael preferred to keep settled.

He stood up, stretching his shoulders, and looked out at the street below. Early commuters shuffled to their cars, and the wet pavement gleamed under the morning light, scattered with puddles that would soon dry up, boundaries disappearing and reforming with each passing car.

Michael knew that if he didn't say something, his resentment would build like pressure behind a dam. And when the dam finally broke, the aftermath wouldn't be pretty. Past experiences had taught him that keeping his mouth shut only led to walls between people, walls too high to see over. He didn't want that with James.

By mid-morning, Michael was in his workshop, surrounded by planks of wood and the scent of fresh-cut cedar and varnish. Here, everything made sense. He could shape, measure, and control his surroundings, unlike the unpredictable dynamics with his family. He picked up a chisel, testing its edge against a block of oak, grounding himself in the task. As he worked, he rehearsed what he would say to James, hoping to strike the right balance—firm but not aggressive, direct but not hurtful. "Look, James," he thought, rehearsing, "I need some boundaries when it comes to my space."

The sudden shrill ring of his phone jolted him back. He wiped his hands on his worn apron and glanced at the screen—James. He took a deep breath, letting the familiar scents of the shop steady him, and picked up.

"Hey, Mike!" James's voice was loud, casual, brimming with energy. "Thought I'd swing by later, bring some beers, catch up."

Michael felt his pulse quicken. *Now's the time,* he thought. Clearing his throat, he spoke carefully, choosing each word like he would select the right tool for the job.

"That sounds good, James," he said, keeping his tone steady, "but can we set some ground rules?" There was a pause on the other end, the kind that hung in the air, heavy with anticipation. Michael pressed on. "I need a bit more notice before you come by. It's just... I need my time and space. It's important to me."

There was a beat of silence before James finally spoke, his voice quieter but not defensive. "Yeah… yeah, I get that, Mike. I didn't mean to crowd you. I just thought it was good, you know? Us hanging out."

Relieved, Michael softened. "I get that too, man. I just need to know that when I say 'I need some space,' it's respected. That's all."

They talked a bit more, hashing out what worked for both of them. By the end, Michael felt a weight lift, the kind of relief that comes from knowing you've spoken up for yourself without tearing someone else down.

As dusk settled over the city, Michael found himself back in his workshop, watching the last rays of light stretch across the floor, casting long shadows on the wooden planks he'd spent the day shaping. He thought about how setting boundaries was like building something—measure twice, cut once. Done right, boundaries weren't walls; they were bridges, making relationships stronger and more resilient.

He leaned back against his workbench, crossing his arms, and allowed himself a rare, satisfied smile. Turns out, crafting boundaries wasn't all that different from woodworking. It took patience, precision, and the guts to make the first cut.

In the end, maybe these boundaries would be the thing that allowed his relationship with James to thrive, not just survive.

Who's in Charge? Setting Boundaries Like a Boss

Boundaries are not just lines drawn on a map; they are essential frameworks in our lives that dictate how others can treat us and how we treat ourselves. For many men, especially when healing from deep emotional wounds such as those with maternal origins, learning to set healthy boundaries is not just an act of self-care—it's a revolutionary act of reclaiming power.

Boundary setting is crucial for emotional well-being because it helps manage the input and output of our emotional energy. It prevents our resources from being depleted by external demands and checks the intrusion of negative influences into our personal space. This chapter dives deep into why boundaries are not selfish but necessary, how to effectively establish them, and the transformative impact they can have on your relationships.

The first lesson here is straightforward: **boundaries are essential for maintaining your mental health**. They help you define what you are comfortable with and how you wish to be treated by others. This clarity is the foundation of all healthy interactions. Without it, we risk letting others overwrite our needs with their expectations, leading to stress, resentment, and burnout.

Next, we tackle the 'how'. **Setting boundaries is an art**—one that involves clear communication and the courage to stand up for your needs even when pressured to relent. It's about expressing your needs respectfully but firmly, ensuring that you are heard and understood. This might feel uncomfortable initially, especially if you're not used to asserting yourself, but like any skill, it gets easier with practice.

Implementing these boundaries effectively transforms relationships by fostering mutual respect and safety. When both parties understand and honor each other's limits, interactions become more thoughtful and empowering. This doesn't just apply to new relationships but also to existing ones that may need recalibration.

Step Up: Boundary Setting Mastery

Let's face it, setting boundaries might not sound like the most exciting skill to master, but here's the truth: boundaries are the foundation of every healthy relationship—whether it's with your boss, your brother, or even yourself. Think of it like putting up a sturdy fence around your yard: it keeps the good stuff in, the unwanted out, and makes it clear where you stand. Let's break it down in a way that resonates with the guy you are and the guy you want to become.

---

1. Reflect on Your Emotional Needs
Grab a quiet moment, your favorite drink, and think about what pushes your buttons or drains your energy. Is it that coworker who always piles their work on you? The buddy who turns up unannounced? Pinpoint the areas where you

feel stretched too thin. This step is like scouting the terrain before you build—know where the weak spots are so you can shore them up.

---

2. Communicate Your Boundaries Clearly

Here's the deal: people aren't mind readers. If you want them to respect your space, you need to spell it out. Use direct, no-BS language. For example: "Hey, I'm not available after 8 PM for work calls—it's my family time." Don't sugarcoat it, and don't over-explain. You're not asking for permission; you're stating your needs.

---

3. Be Firm and Consistent

Boundaries without follow-through are like locks without keys—useless. If you say no to working weekends, don't suddenly say yes because someone pushes harder. Consistency isn't about being stubborn; it's about showing people you mean what you say. If they test your limits (and they will), hold your ground.

---

4. Practice Self-Care

You can't enforce boundaries if you're running on empty.

Take care of yourself first—whether that's hitting the gym, playing a round of golf, meditating, or just unplugging for a while. Think of self-care as recharging your battery so you have the energy to stand up for yourself when it matters most.

---

5. Address Violations Promptly
When someone crosses the line, don't let it slide. Speak up immediately and remind them of the boundary you've set. "Hey, I mentioned I wasn't taking calls after 8 PM. Let's stick to that." Silence often gets interpreted as approval, so nip it in the bud before it becomes a pattern.

---

6. Seek Backup When Needed
Sometimes, boundary setting feels like trying to bench press more weight than you're ready for—and that's okay. If it's tough, talk to a mentor, coach, or even a therapist. Getting an outside perspective can help you strengthen your approach and build confidence.

---

7. Adjust the Fence as Needed
Life evolves, and so do your boundaries. What worked when

you were single might not fit when you're in a relationship or have kids. Periodically check in with yourself to make sure your boundaries match your current priorities. It's not about being rigid—it's about staying aligned with who you are now.

---

8. Be Assertive, Not Aggressive

You can enforce your boundaries without turning it into a cage fight. The goal isn't to bulldoze people—it's to make your needs clear while respecting theirs. Speak firmly but respectfully, like a coach who knows how to push the team without tearing them down.

Every time you set a boundary, you're not just saying "no" to someone else—you're saying "yes" to yourself. And that's a win worth celebrating. This isn't about being selfish or difficult; it's about creating a life where your energy, time, and peace are protected.

Boundaries aren't walls; they're bridges to healthier relationships and a stronger, happier version of you. Step up, take the reins, and start building the life you deserve—one boundary at a time.

Part One: *Understanding the Importance of Boundaries for Emotional Well-Being*

Boundaries in relationships are like the rules of a basketball game; they create a framework that allows the game to be played safely and enjoyably. Without boundaries, or rules, chaos ensues, and no one benefits. Similarly, setting personal boundaries is crucial for maintaining emotional health and ensuring interactions with others are respectful and fulfilling.

Every individual has their own set of emotional needs and limits. Recognizing these is the first step towards establishing boundaries. It's about knowing what you can tolerate and accept as well as what makes you feel uncomfortable or stressed. These boundaries aren't just about saying no; they're about creating a space for yourself where you can thrive emotionally.

Consider this: when someone consistently oversteps your limits, it can lead to feelings of resentment, anger, or even sadness. These emotions are signals, indicating that your boundaries are being violated. Just as a basketball player calls a foul when a rule is broken, you must identify and communicate your emotional limits.

Boundary setting is not about pushing people away but rather about building relationships on a foundation of mutual respect. It involves clear communication of one's needs and expectations to others. This clarity helps prevent misunderstandings and ensures that both parties feel valued and understood in the relationship.

Boundaries are essential for protecting our emotional space and ensuring our interactions with others are healthy and respectful.

Part Two: *Learning How to Set and Assert Healthy Boundaries*

Setting boundaries is an art that requires clarity, consistency, and courage. First, it's important to clearly understand what your own needs are in any given relationship — be it with family, friends, or romantic partners. Knowing what you value most helps in drawing lines more confidently.

Imagine setting boundaries like setting up a fence around a prized garden; the fence protects the garden from pests while still allowing sunlight and rain to nurture its growth. In personal terms, boundaries protect your values and mental health without isolating you from meaningful connections.

The process of asserting boundaries can often stir up

discomfort, especially if you're not used to standing up for yourself. It may involve saying no more often than saying yes, or asking for space in situations where you used to offer unlimited time and energy. This shift might surprise people who've known the 'old' you — the one who didn't prioritize his own needs.

Effective communication is key when setting boundaries. It's not just about what you say; it's how you say it. Being assertive means expressing your needs clearly and respectfully without aggression or passivity. Think of it as stating the rules of that basketball game not at the top of your lungs but with firmness and directness.

Remember, setting boundaries is a dynamic process. As your life evolves, so too might your needs and limits change. Regular check-ins with yourself are crucial to ensure your boundaries still serve their purpose.

Could reflecting on moments when you felt overwhelmed help identify where you need stronger boundaries?

Part Three: *Implementing Boundaries to Foster Respect and Safety in Relationships*

The Boundary Setting Framework (BSF)

The "Boundary Setting Framework" (BSF) tailored for individuals dealing with emotional scars from maternal relationships consists of three phases: Identification, Communication, and Maintenance.

Identification

In the Identification phase, the focus is on recognizing personal limits based on one's values, beliefs, and emotional needs. This phase requires deep self-reflection to pinpoint areas where past interactions may have encroached upon one's sense of autonomy or safety. Identifying these limits is akin to understanding what parts of the garden need the most protection.

Communication

Next is the Communication phase which outlines strategies for articulating these boundaries assertively to others without aggression or passivity. This could include language templates such as "I feel [emotion] when you [behavior], I need [change]." This approach helps in conveying boundaries in a manner that respects both parties involved.

Maintenance

Lastly, Maintenance encompasses ongoing adjustments to one's boundaries in response to new situations or relationships while reaffirming existing ones. It's similar to checking fences for weak spots or potential breaches regularly — a necessary step to ensure continued protection.

Each component of this framework interacts symbiotically: identification informs communication which then shapes maintenance efforts; each part supports another like beams in a sturdy building structure.

Implementing BSF not only helps manage interactions stemming from past maternal wounds but also fortifies one's emotional health against future disturbances by reinforcing personal respect and safety within all types of relationships.

Maintaining healthy boundaries reinforces self-respect while ensuring our relationships are mutually beneficially respectful

Setting boundaries isn't just a fancy term for keeping people at arm's length; it's your emotional armor in the battlefield of life. Understanding the critical role of boundaries for your emotional well-being is like unlocking a new level in the game of life where you're finally in control. It's about knowing when to say yes and, more importantly, having the courage to say no without feeling guilty.

Let's face it: asserting boundaries can feel like you're the bad guy sometimes. But remember, it's less about pushing others away and more about pulling your own well-being closer. Every time you set a boundary, you're telling yourself and the world that your feelings, time, and energy are valuable. This isn't just self-care—it's self-respect.

Now, implementing these boundaries is where the rubber meets the road. It's not enough to know what lines need drawing; the real magic happens when you consistently enforce them. This is where safety and respect become more than just concepts—they become palpable elements that enhance every relationship in your life. Whether it's with family, friends, or even colleagues, clear boundaries help prevent misunderstandings and foster a healthier, more respectful environment.

So here's the kicker: boundaries are not walls to keep people out but gates to let the right ones in. They help filter out what doesn't serve you and keep what enriches you. Embracing this practice means stepping into a world where your emotional health is protected, allowing you to engage more deeply and authentically with those around you.

As we move forward on this journey of healing and connection, remember that setting boundaries is not a one-off event but a dynamic process of tuning in to your evolving needs and relationships. It requires bravery, consistency, and yes—a bit of sass! So stand firm but kind; be bold but compassionate. After all, it's your life's story—make sure it's written on your terms.

Embrace your power to shape your interactions and protect your peace. It's not just about making space for yourself; it's about making space for healthier relationships that truly honor who you are.

As we wrap up this chapter on setting boundaries, carry forward this toolkit of awareness, assertion, and action. Let these tools empower you to cultivate an environment where mutual respect and emotional safety aren't just hoped for—they're expected. Remember: You're not alone on this journey; every step towards boundary-setting is a step towards healing not just yourself but also nurturing those authentic connections that make life worth living.

So go ahead—set those boundaries with confidence! Your future self will thank you for it.

Chapter 8: Conversations that Heal

The park buzzed with life—kids laughing by the fountain, a group of joggers pacing through the trails, and the faint sound of someone strumming a guitar under a tree. Michael sat on a weathered wooden bench, his elbows resting on his knees as he watched the chess players scattered across the checkered tables. The sun filtered through the leaves, casting shifting shadows over his hands and the book lying forgotten in his lap.

His mind wasn't on the park or the game. It was replaying the conversation he'd had with James the night before. Their voices had clashed again, echoing years of unresolved tension. James's sharp words still rang in his ears, striking chords that were too familiar. Michael wasn't just frustrated—he was tired. Tired of the same old patterns, the same walls they kept running into.

Nearby, a young boy chased a butterfly, his laughter ringing out as he darted back and forth. Michael couldn't help but smile faintly at the simplicity of it all. He envied that kind of freedom—freedom to feel, to express, without the weight of expectations or pride holding you back.

Michael leaned back, staring at the canopy above him. He thought about what his therapist had said during their last session: *"Healing doesn't happen in isolation, Michael. It happens through dialogue. But that dialogue has to be clear, honest, and compassionate—for both parties."*

That was the part that stuck with him: *compassionate*. He realized he'd been too focused on defending himself, on being heard, without truly listening to James's side of things. Conversations that heal aren't about "winning" or "losing." They're about connection.

An elderly man sat down beside him, pulling out a chessboard with a nod. "Care for a game?" he asked, his voice calm and inviting.

Michael hesitated, then nodded. "Sure."

The man, who introduced himself as Henry, set up the board with practiced ease. As they played, Henry shared snippets of wisdom. "Chess is like life," he said, moving his knight. "Sometimes the best move isn't the obvious one. Sometimes, it's the one that makes you pause and think about the bigger picture."

Michael chuckled. "Sounds like you've been through a few

tough games."

Henry grinned. "Haven't we all?"

As the game unfolded, Michael reflected on his relationship with James. He thought about how many of their conversations were like chess matches—both of them trying to outmaneuver the other instead of working toward mutual understanding.

By the time the game ended (and Henry won), Michael felt a rare clarity settle over him. Healing his relationship with James wasn't just about what *he* needed to say—it was about what *they* needed to share.

Walking home, Michael drafted the conversation in his mind, imagining a dialogue where he spoke not to defend but to understand. The thought of trying again didn't feel as daunting anymore.

Conversations that heal aren't easy, but they're worth it. They're the bridges that connect pain to understanding, isolation to connection. And for the first time in a long time, Michael felt ready to take the first step across.

Unlocking the Power of Words: Heal and Connect

Mastering the art of communication is not just about talking; it's about opening doors to a deeper understanding and connection, especially when it comes to healing deep-rooted emotional wounds. In the journey to mend the maternal wound—a scar left from strained or dysfunctional mother-son relationships—effective dialogue plays a pivotal role. It's not just about saying what you feel, but how you say it that can turn conversations into bridges of healing.

The essence of healing through conversation lies in **expressing needs and boundaries clearly**. Many men struggle with voicing their innermost feelings and setting clear boundaries because they fear being vulnerable or misunderstood. However, cultivating these communication skills is crucial for emotional health and relationship building. It empowers you to articulate your emotions without aggression or passivity, striking a balance that fosters respect and understanding.

Moreover, enhancing emotional intimacy is another significant milestone achieved through effective communication. It's about creating a safe space where both parties feel seen and heard. This chapter delves into how nurturing **clear and compassionate dialogue** can deepen connections, making them more fulfilling. Emotional intimacy isn't just about sharing joys; it's also about having the courage to share the pains, the fears, and the doubts, knowing that your words will be met with empathy rather than judgment.

Misunderstandings can often escalate into conflicts that might seem insurmountable. However, by honing assertive communication skills, you can **prevent these misunderstandings** before they grow. Assertiveness allows you to express your point of view firmly and fairly, without stepping on anyone else's toes. This chapter offers practical advice on how to cultivate this skill, which not only helps in personal relationships but also in professional settings.

The journey towards healing is like rebuilding a house where every conversation adds a brick of trust and understanding. Think of each dialogue as an opportunity to reinforce the foundation of your relationships. The stronger the foundation, the more resilient your relationships will be against the storms of miscommunication and conflict.

This exploration isn't just about talking through problems but transforming how you connect with others at a fundamental level. It involves peeling back layers of past hurts and misconceptions to reveal a core of authenticity and vulnerability. By embracing this vulnerability in conversations, you create a space for genuine connection and profound healing.

Lastly, remember that this journey is not a sprint but a marathon. Improving your communication skills takes consistent effort and practice. Each step forward is a step towards not just healing the maternal wound but also towards building lasting relationships rooted in mutual respect and understanding.

In embracing these principles, you are not just healing; you're evolving into someone who can foster healthier, more authentic connections with everyone around you—connections that uplift, nurture, and sustain.

Mastering Communication Skills: Say What You Mean, Get What You Need

Let's cut to the chase—communicating your needs and setting boundaries isn't always easy, especially for men who've been raised to "man up" and keep emotions bottled up. But here's the thing: effective communication isn't just about talking; it's about being heard, understood, and respected. And trust me, once you master this, it's a game-changer—not just in your relationships but in your confidence and self-respect.

Imagine trying to play a card game with your buddy, but you

don't know the rules. Frustrating, right? That's what relationships feel like when communication isn't clear. By learning to express your needs and boundaries effectively, you're essentially writing the rulebook for how others interact with you. Clear communication isn't just about avoiding misunderstandings—it's about building mutual respect and trust.

Communication is More Than Words

Think of communication like a workout—it's not just about one move; it's about the whole routine. Sure, the words you choose matter, but so do other factors:

- Timing: Don't drop heavy conversations in the middle of a chaotic moment. Choose the right time when both you and the other person are calm and focused.
- Tone: The difference between "I need some space" and "I NEED SOME SPACE" is massive. Stay calm, firm, and respectful.
- Body Language: Your posture, eye contact, and even your hands say as much as your words. Slouching or crossing your arms? That screams defensiveness. Open posture? That's confidence.

Communication is a dance, and if you're out of sync, the whole thing can fall apart. Pay attention to how the other person reacts and adjust your approach if needed. The goal isn't to dominate the conversation but to make it flow.

The Power of Assertiveness

Here's where most guys get tripped up—they either go full-blown aggressive or completely passive. Assertiveness is the sweet spot in the middle. It's about stating your needs and boundaries clearly without being a jerk or a pushover.

For example, instead of saying, "You're always in my space, and it's driving me nuts," try, "I value my alone time, and I'd appreciate it if you could check in before dropping by." See the difference? You're being direct but respectful, firm but kind.

Make It a Habit

Like hitting the gym or learning a new skill, communication gets easier the more you practice. Start small—maybe with a coworker or friend—and work your way up to tougher conversations. With time, you'll not only get better at expressing yourself but also at understanding others.

Why This Matters

Think about the best relationships in your life. Chances are, they thrive on mutual respect and understanding. That's what mastering communication gives you—it sets the foundation for stronger connections, less drama, and more peace of mind.

So, step up. Learn the dance. Start setting the rules for how others treat you. Because when you can communicate your needs and boundaries effectively, you're not just surviving life's challenges—you're owning them.

Enhancing Emotional Intimacy Through Clear and Compassionate Dialogue

Emotional intimacy isn't built overnight—it's earned through trust, understanding, and, most importantly, clear communication. For men, this might feel like unfamiliar territory, but the truth is, meaningful conversations can be as grounding as a solid workout or as satisfying as a well-earned victory. Communication that goes beyond surface-level small talk and into the realm of feelings can strengthen connections in ways that silence or assumptions never will.

Clear dialogue starts with transparency. Being open about your thoughts and emotions isn't about weakness; it's about strength—the kind that invites the people you care about to truly know you. Think of it as cracking open a window to let fresh air in. Vulnerability can be uncomfortable, but it's also refreshing and necessary for closeness.

Compassion takes this transparency to the next level. When you craft your words with honesty *and* consideration for the other person's feelings, it shows respect. This combination builds bridges between your experience and theirs—a pathway to mutual understanding.

==Questions act as bridges==—they connect your curiosity to someone else's perspective. When you ask thoughtful questions, it's like saying, "I value your story enough to want to understand it." For example, instead of assuming why someone feels a certain way, you could ask, "Can you help me understand what's been weighing on you lately?" These bridges create opportunities to deepen emotional bonds and dismantle potential barriers before they become walls.

Now imagine this: You and a loved one often butt heads over miscommunication. Maybe it's assumptions or half-listened responses that light the fuse. By embracing clarity and compassion, you can shift the focus from conflict to connection. Suddenly, the dialogue isn't about "winning" but about working together.

Sometimes, metaphors help simplify emotions that are hard to explain. For instance, describing emotional exhaustion as "carrying a backpack filled with stones" instantly conveys a sense of heaviness without requiring a lengthy explanation.

These tools make your inner world more accessible to others, fostering understanding and empathy.

Could seeing your emotional dialogues as opportunities to paint clearer pictures of your inner world lead to more profound intimacy? Absolutely.

Prevent Misunderstandings and Strengthen Connections Through Assertive Communication

Assertive communication isn't just about making yourself heard—it's about cutting through the noise and ensuring your message lands with clarity and respect. Misunderstandings often arise when words are vague or loaded with assumptions. Being assertive is like aiming an arrow straight at a target—precise, intentional, and hard to misinterpret.

When you express yourself assertively, you reduce the chances of your words being twisted or diluted. You're not just throwing out a vague "I'm fine" when you're clearly not—you're saying, "I'm feeling overwhelmed, and I need some time to decompress."

Here's the kicker: assertiveness doesn't mean bulldozing the other person. It's about balancing confidence with respect, ensuring your voice is heard without dismissing theirs.

Compassionate Communication Model

This structured approach is especially useful when healing relational wounds, whether they stem from maternal issues or other deep-seated conflicts. Think of it as a framework to keep tough conversations on track:

1. **Active Listening**
   Don't just hear the words—listen to the meaning behind them. Focus on what the speaker is really saying instead of mentally preparing your response. A nod, a simple "I hear you," or a thoughtful follow-up can go a long way in building trust.

2. **Empathy Expression**
   After listening, show you're connecting emotionally with what's been said. Even if you don't agree, you can say, "I can see why that would make you feel frustrated." Empathy isn't about fixing—it's about acknowledging.

3. **Assertive Speaking**
   This is your time to speak your truth without aggression or passivity. Statements like, "I need space to focus in the mornings," are clear and respectful. Assertiveness ensures your needs are voiced and valued.

4. **Feedback Integration**
   Treat feedback as insight, not criticism. When the

other person responds, don't dismiss their perspective. Instead, use it to refine your understanding of the situation and move the conversation forward.

Each of these components links together seamlessly, forming a communication cycle that fosters deeper connections and mutual respect. Active listening leads to empathy, which makes assertiveness easier, and incorporating feedback ensures the conversation feels like a collaboration rather than a confrontation.

Building Stronger Bridges

Effective communication is more than just avoiding misunderstandings—it's about creating opportunities for deeper connection. Each conversation is a chance to build trust, understanding, and respect.

Think of your words as either bricks in a wall or steps on a bridge. When you choose compassion and clarity, you're not just talking—you're creating pathways that strengthen your relationships and, ultimately, yourself.

So, here's your challenge: Start seeing every dialogue as a fresh opportunity to connect, to tweak your approach, and to strengthen the bonds that matter most. When you embrace these skills, you're not just having conversations—you're mastering the art of meaningful connection, one step, one word, and one question at a time.

Chapter 9: Leaning on Trustworthy Shoulders

The kitchen smelled of simmering garlic and herbs, the kind of scent that clung to the air and felt like home. Marcus stood by the sink, peeling potatoes with practiced ease. His hands moved rhythmically, guided by years of repetition, as he stared out the window. The laughter of kids playing tag drifted in, mingling with the low hum of the city beyond.

The sound tugged at something deep within him. He thought about his mother, about how her laughter used to light up their small apartment like the sun breaking through a cloudy day. It had been years since they'd spoken—years since misunderstandings and unresolved pain had created a chasm too wide for either of them to cross.

He paused, gripping the potato in his hand, as memories flooded back: her standing over the stove, humming along to old soul records, or the way she'd ruffle his hair after a hard day at school. There had been warmth once, a connection. Now, it felt as distant as the kids' laughter outside, drifting away on the breeze.

Last week, during a chess game in the park, James had

planted a seed in his mind. "You can't carry all this on your own, man," he had said, his voice calm but firm as he moved a rook into position. "You need people who've been through it—people who get it."

At the time, Marcus had brushed it off with a shrug, muttering something about handling his own problems. But the truth was, James's words lingered. There was something in them he couldn't ignore. Maybe leaning on others wasn't a sign of weakness; maybe it was exactly what he needed to take the first step toward healing.

As he rinsed his hands under the cool tap water, Marcus felt the beginnings of resolve forming within him. He didn't have to have all the answers yet, but he could at least start looking. Therapy? A support group? Just the thought of sharing his story with strangers made his chest tighten, but it also stirred a small flicker of hope.

Later that evening, Marcus found himself flipping through an old photo album he had tucked away in the back of a cabinet. The pages felt brittle, each one holding fragments of a life he hadn't revisited in years. One picture stopped him cold: his mother, beaming proudly at his high school graduation, her arms wrapped around his shoulders. Her smile was so big, so genuine, that it made his heart ache.

He traced a finger over the image, remembering the joy of

that day—and the tension that had followed soon after. The memory was bittersweet, heavy with the weight of everything left unsaid. Could they ever get back to that place?

Leaning back on the couch, Marcus closed the album and rested his head against the cushions. He let his mind wander, imagining a future where they could talk again without the barriers of anger and regret. Where understanding could flow freely, not just between them, but between him and others who carried similar wounds.

The thought wasn't just about reconciling with his mother. It was about finding his tribe—people who could listen, share, and understand without judgment. People who could help him shoulder the weight he had carried alone for too long.

Before heading to bed, Marcus pulled out his phone and typed "support groups for estranged family relationships" into the search bar. He didn't press enter right away. Instead, he sat there, staring at the screen, his thumb hovering over the button. This was new territory, and it scared him—but it also felt like the right direction.

As he finally hit "search," Marcus let out a long breath. This wasn't just about healing his relationship with his mother. It was about healing himself. And maybe, just maybe, he didn't have to do it alone.

Trust, Marcus realized, wasn't just about others—it was about believing in the possibility of something better. And with that thought, he allowed himself a small, hopeful smile.

Who's Got Your Back? The Art of Building Your Healing Squad

Healing from maternal wounds isn't a solo mission—it's a team sport. Think of it like preparing for the biggest fight of your life. You wouldn't step into the ring without a coach, sparring partners, and a crew cheering you on from the sidelines. The same goes for emotional healing. This isn't just about finding people to vent to; it's about surrounding yourself with folks who get it—people who'll push you to grow, lend a hand when you stumble, and keep you grounded when things get tough.

Building your healing squad is about more than just identifying a few close friends or family members. It's about creating a circle of people who bring out the best in you, challenge you to look at things differently, and hold you accountable in ways that matter. Whether it's a friend who calls you out on your BS, a sibling who listens without judgment, or a therapist who helps you untangle the knots in your mind, the right support makes all the difference.

Reaching out might feel awkward or heavy at first, like lifting a hundred-pound dumbbell without a warm-up. But here's the truth: admitting you need help is one of the strongest things you can do. And when you let others in, you're not just sharing the weight—you're inviting them to be part of your journey.

Step-by-Step: Crafting Your Circle

Here's how you build a squad that has your back, no matter what:

---

1. Identify the Real Ones
Look around your life and think about the people who make you feel safe, respected, and understood. These are the friends who actually *listen*, the family members who don't judge, and the mentors who offer solid advice. It's not about quantity—it's about quality.

---

2. Make the First Move
Reaching out can feel uncomfortable, but someone has to start the conversation. Shoot that text, make that call, or grab a coffee with someone you trust. Let them know you're working through some stuff and that you value their perspective. Don't worry about getting it perfect—just get it

started.

---

3. Be Clear About Your Needs
Once you've got their attention, tell them what kind of support you're looking for. Maybe you need someone to listen without offering solutions. Maybe you need advice, encouragement, or even just a distraction when things get too heavy. When you're clear about what you need, it's easier for them to show up in the right way.

---

4. Lock in Regular Check-Ins
Healing isn't a one-time conversation. Schedule time to connect regularly, whether it's a weekly phone call, a monthly hangout, or even just a quick check-in text. Consistency keeps the support strong and reminds you that you're not alone in this.

---

5. Get Real—The Good and the Bad
Don't just share the highlight reel. True healing means being honest about your wins *and* your setbacks. Let your squad see the full picture—they're here to support the whole you,

not just the polished version.

---

6. Bring in the Pros

Sometimes your friends and family aren't enough, and that's okay. A therapist or counselor specializing in familial issues can provide the tools and insights you need to go deeper in your healing. Think of them as the coach who keeps you sharp and focused.

---

7. Keep It Healthy

Even the best support systems need boundaries. Make sure your interactions stay balanced and don't drain anyone—including yourself. Healthy relationships are about give and take, not constant taking.

---

8. Say Thank You

Support is a two-way street, and gratitude goes a long way. Let your squad know how much you appreciate their time and effort. Whether it's a heartfelt thank-you, a small gesture, or just being there for them when they need it, showing appreciation strengthens those bonds.

Why Your Squad Matters

No man is an island, and that's especially true when it comes to healing wounds as deep as maternal ones. Your squad isn't just there to listen or nod along—they're there to challenge you, cheer you on, and remind you of your worth when you lose sight of it.

By surrounding yourself with people who genuinely care, you're not just building a network—you're building a community that lifts you up and keeps you moving forward. These connections don't just help you heal—they help you grow. They turn your struggles into wisdom, your pain into purpose, and your isolation into belonging.

So, take that first step. Reach out. Build your team. Because every step you take with the right support is a step toward transformation—and you're stronger with your squad behind you.

Identifying Supportive Individuals

When embarking on a journey to heal from maternal wounds, the first crucial step is to identify supportive individuals who can provide aid and comfort. This isn't just about finding someone who will listen; it's about connecting with those who truly understand and empathize with your struggles. These could be friends who have faced similar issues, family members who are emotionally available, or professionals like therapists or counselors who specialize in this area.

Imagine your support system as a basketball team where every player has a vital role. Just as a point guard facilitates the game, making strategic plays, a good therapist guides you through your healing process. Similarly, friends and family can be like forwards and centers, protecting you and offering the emotional rebounds you need when times get tough.

The process of selecting these individuals should be approached with intentionality. It's important to evaluate the trustworthiness and empathy levels of potential supporters. Consider their history of confidentiality, willingness to listen without judgment, and ability to provide constructive feedback. A strong support network isn't necessarily large but is profoundly attuned to your emotional frequencies.

Building this network involves reaching out and sometimes being vulnerable about your needs and experiences. It might feel daunting at first, but opening up can strengthen bonds and foster a deeper understanding among those around you. Remember, vulnerability is not a sign of weakness but a courageous step towards healing.

Key point: *Identify trustworthy individuals who resonate with your emotional journey and are capable of providing the support you need.*

Utilizing Your Support System

Once you've identified your support team, the next step is utilizing this network effectively for insights and emotional relief. Regular interactions with your support system can provide fresh perspectives on personal challenges that seem insurmountable when faced alone. These interactions act as a mirror reflecting not only your struggles but also paths to overcoming them.

Think of each conversation with a friend or session with a therapist as plugging into a charging station. Each interaction recharges your emotional batteries and equips you with insights to tackle the day-to-day aspects of healing from maternal wounds. Sharing your thoughts and feelings can help clarify them, giving you a clearer road map for navigating your emotions.

However, it's crucial to approach these interactions with openness and receptivity. Be ready to receive advice as well as offer your own insights—support systems work best as two-way streets. The flow of give-and-take ensures all parties feel valued and significant, which strengthens the bonds within this network.

Support isn't just about discussing problems; it's also about celebrating small victories on your healing journey. These celebrations can be incredibly uplifting and serve as reminders of the progress you're making, no matter how incremental it may seem.

Could opening up more frequently in safe spaces enrich not just your healing process but also enhance your everyday peace?

Valuing Communal Understanding

The final piece of the puzzle in healing from maternal wounds lies in valuing communal understanding and validation. There's immense power in knowing that you're not alone in your struggles—that others have walked similar paths and emerged stronger on the other side.

Communal understanding fosters a sense of belonging that many find missing when dealing with personal traumas alone. This shared experience forms an unspoken bond that can be incredibly comforting during tough times.

Consider communal validation like sunlight after days of stormy weather—it doesn't change what happened but provides warmth that starts mending what felt broken inside. When someone else validates our feelings or experiences, it reassures us that our emotions are real and legitimate.

In practical terms, engaging in group therapy sessions or community support groups where stories and experiences are exchanged can significantly amplify this sense of shared understanding. These settings offer unique opportunities for learning from others' coping mechanisms while providing space to share your own insights.

Valuing communal understanding helps solidify personal healing by affirming that one's feelings are both shared and significant.

Bringing It All Together

To navigate the complex terrain of healing from maternal wounds effectively, one must first identify supportive individuals keenly attuned to their emotional needs; utilize these relationships for continuous insight and emotional sustenance; and appreciate the communal validation that reinforces one's personal experiences within a broader narrative. This holistic approach ensures not just survival but thriving beyond one's foundational scars.

Leaning on trustworthy shoulders isn't just a good idea; it's a game changer in healing. Let's face it, walking through the healing process can sometimes feel like you're trying to solve a Rubik's cube blindfolded. But why struggle alone when you can have a squad of supporters guiding your hands? Identifying supportive individuals is like assembling your personal dream team. These are the folks who won't just nod and smile, but will genuinely dive into the trenches with you, helping you sort through the emotional maze.

Utilizing your support system effectively is where the magic happens. It's one thing to have people ready to back you up, and another to actually let them in on the play-by-play of your healing journey. Think of it this way: if life were a basketball game, your support system are the teammates passing you the ball and cheering every basket. They offer insights that might not strike you when you're flying solo and provide emotional relief that's as comforting as grandma's house on a Sunday afternoon.

The value of communal understanding and validation in this healing process cannot be overstated. It's about more than just feeling heard; it's about feeling understood on a soul-deep level. When others validate your feelings and experiences, it's like putting wind in your sails on those days when the sea seems too rough. This shared understanding not only fortifies your own healing but knits stronger bonds within your community.

So, remember: **healing is not a solitary journey**. It's rich with opportunities for connection, growth, and deep, meaningful exchanges that enrich both the giver and receiver. As we gear up for the next chapter in this journey, keep leaning into those relationships that empower and uplift you. After all, every superhero needs a sidekick or two—or maybe an entire league! Here's to forging ahead with resilience, determination, and a squad that's got your back every step of the way!

Chapter 10: Reclaiming the Narrative: A New Dawn

The city park buzzed with life—joggers pacing along gravel paths, kids chasing one another around the fountain, and the occasional bark of a dog slicing through the air. Michael sat on a worn wooden bench, his elbows resting on his knees, staring out at the chess players scattered across the checkered tables like pieces on a giant board. The sun filtered through the trees, casting shifting patterns on his weathered hands and the dog-eared book he'd barely glanced at in the past half hour.

He wasn't there to read. He was there to think.

Michael was at a turning point—the kind of moment that feels big, even if no one else can see it. His mind wandered back to his father, the man whose stern voice had been a soundtrack to his childhood. "Man up," his dad would bark whenever he showed fear or frustration, as if emotions were something to be conquered, not felt. Those words had been his compass for years, shaping his choices, his relationships, and the mask he wore.

But now, they felt like chains.

A burst of laughter snapped him out of his thoughts. A boy, no older than eight, was chasing a scrappy dog across the grass, their game of tag punctuated by the dog's playful barks. Michael felt a pang of envy. That boy wasn't thinking about appearances or expectations. He wasn't weighed down by unspoken rules. He was just... free.

Michael exhaled and leaned back, letting the park's energy wash over him. He thought about the book lying forgotten in his lap—a book about rewriting your personal narrative. The words had struck a chord. Healing wasn't about erasing the past; it was about reclaiming it, understanding the pain, and using it to shape something better.

The breeze picked up, flipping the book's pages as if urging him to keep reading, but his attention was drawn to an elderly man shuffling toward his bench. The man carried a weathered chessboard under one arm, his face lined with years but softened by a warm smile.

"Care for a game?" the man asked, his voice steady but inviting.

Michael hesitated for a second before nodding. "Sure. Why

not?"

The man set up the board with practiced ease, the pieces clicking softly as they found their places. Michael stared at the pieces, the familiar shapes suddenly seeming symbolic. Life was a lot like chess, wasn't it? Every move mattered, every decision a step toward something—victory, defeat, or simply survival.

As the game began, they exchanged small talk. The man, whose name was Henry, had been coming to the park for years, playing chess with strangers and sharing snippets of wisdom between moves.

"Life's not so different from this board," Henry said, moving a knight into position. "Sometimes you make bold moves. Other times, you have to play defense. And every now and then, you have to sacrifice something to gain something better."

Michael chuckled. "Not bad advice for a chess game—or life."

The game continued, Michael moving pieces with growing confidence as Henry shared stories of losses that turned into lessons and setbacks that cleared the way for something greater.

"Don't hold onto old strategies just because they worked once," Henry said as he moved his queen. "The game changes, and you've got to change with it."

Michael didn't win the game—not even close—but he didn't feel like he'd lost either. As he shook Henry's hand, he felt a strange sense of clarity. Life wasn't about erasing the past or pretending the pain didn't happen. It was about learning from it, adapting, and making deliberate moves forward.

As Michael walked away, the sun dipped lower in the sky, casting long shadows across the park. He thought about the freedom that little boy had chasing his dog and wondered if he could find something similar—not by running from his pain, but by finally facing it.

Reclaiming his narrative wasn't going to happen overnight. It would take effort, strategy, and probably a few losses along the way. But for the first time in a long time, Michael felt ready to play the game on his own terms.

Could letting go of the past really be about holding on to hope instead? Maybe it wasn't about forgetting or fixing. Maybe it was about choosing, move by move, to create something better. A new dawn. A new story. His story.

Reclaim Your Story, Redefine Your Bonds

Healing isn't just about patching up wounds—it's about reclaiming control, rewriting your narrative, and redefining what it means to connect with others. For men, especially those grappling with the scars of strained maternal relationships, this process isn't a straight path but a transformative journey. It's a journey filled with challenges, yes, but also brimming with opportunities to rebuild, redefine, and rise.

Think of your story as a film that's already been written and directed by someone else. You've played your part, sticking to the script, but now you're holding the camera. It's time to become the director of your own life, to rewrite scenes, recast roles, and create something authentic that reflects the man you are becoming.

Discovering Tools for Healing and Growth

The first step in reclaiming your story is arming yourself with the right tools. Just like a skilled craftsman knows the value of a solid hammer or a sharp saw, emotional healing requires its own set of reliable instruments.

- **Self-Awareness:** This is your foundational tool—the hammer that breaks down emotional walls. It helps you identify what hurts, why it hurts, and how it affects your relationships. Self-awareness isn't about beating yourself up for past mistakes; it's about recognizing them so you can move forward with intention.

- **Open Communication:** Think of this as your level, ensuring your relationships stay balanced and grounded. It's not about talking more—it's about talking honestly. Expressing your feelings clearly and without aggression can shift the dynamics of any connection, transforming misunderstandings into moments of growth.
- **Resilience:** This is your glue and nails, holding everything together when life gets tough. Resilience helps you bounce back from setbacks, face challenges head-on, and keep building—even when the work feels heavy.

These tools aren't quick fixes. They're investments in a stronger, more confident version of yourself.

Rewriting Relationship Narratives

Every man carries a narrative about his relationships—stories shaped by experiences, expectations, and old patterns. But here's the good news: you're not stuck with the script you've been handed.

Imagine your life as a play where you've always been an actor reciting lines someone else wrote. Now, you're the playwright. What scenes would you change? What roles would you recast? Rewriting your narrative means taking control of the story, breaking free from unhealthy patterns, and creating space for healthier dynamics.

Start by identifying the "typos" in your script—those harmful patterns that keep playing out. Maybe it's shutting down during conflict or avoiding vulnerability because it feels risky. Spotting these patterns is the first step toward rewriting them.

Next, focus on the "rewrites." This might mean replacing old habits with new ones, like practicing active listening or sharing appreciation more often. Small changes in your interactions can create ripple effects, leading to stronger, more fulfilling connections.

Rewriting your narrative isn't about erasing the past. It's about choosing a new way forward, one chapter at a time.

Cultivating Meaningful Connections

Authentic connections are built when you're willing to drop the heavy baggage of past traumas. Imagine each unresolved wound as a suitcase you've been dragging around. It's time to open those suitcases, sort through their contents, and decide what to keep and what to leave behind.

Forgiveness plays a crucial role here—not just forgiving others, but forgiving yourself for past mistakes. Letting go of resentment lightens your load, making room for growth and deeper relationships.

Another key ingredient? Vulnerability. Being real with others—not pretending to have it all together—creates the kind of bonds that weather any storm. Vulnerability isn't weakness; it's bravery in its purest form.

Finally, maintaining meaningful connections requires effort. Relationships are like gardens—they need consistent care. Water them with kindness, pull out the weeds of misunderstandings, and give them the sunlight of your time and attention.

Reclaiming the Narrative

As we near the end of this journey, it's clear that reclaiming your story isn't about perfection. It's about progress. Every step forward, no matter how small, is a victory. Healing isn't linear, and it's not always pretty, but it's worth every moment of effort.

Take a moment to reflect on how far you've come. You've delved into the roots of your pain, equipped yourself with tools for growth, and started rewriting the script of your relationships. Each step has brought you closer to a life filled with authenticity, connection, and purpose.

This isn't just about mending what's broken. It's about creating something new—relationships that lift you up, connections that bring you peace, and a life that feels true to who you are.

What Comes Next?

The journey doesn't end here. Keep flexing those emotional muscles. Keep nurturing the connections that matter most. And keep rewriting your story—because the best chapters are yet to come.

Every day is a chance to choose courage over fear, growth over stagnation, and connection over isolation. As you move forward, remember this: your story isn't written by your past. It's shaped by your present actions and your vision for the future.

So go ahead—pick up the pen and write something extraordinary. Your narrative is yours to own, and it's going to be one hell of a story.

Epilogue: Writing the Next Chapter

As we bring this journey to a close, let's take a moment to honor the work you've done. You've confronted past pain, explored the roots of emotional scars, and equipped yourself with tools to transform those wounds into wisdom. This hasn't been a light read; it's been a deep dive into the parts of yourself you might have avoided for years. That takes guts.

Through these pages, we've uncovered the power of understanding your emotional scars, the strength of building authentic connections, and the liberation that comes with rewriting your narrative. The insights you've gained aren't just theories—they're your map forward, guiding you toward healthier relationships, greater self-awareness, and a more fulfilling life.

But here's the thing: this isn't the end. This is the beginning. Healing is an ongoing process, and every day presents an opportunity to take another step toward the life you want to live.

Main Ideas Revisited

Let's recap the key themes we've explored together:

- **Understanding Emotional Scars**: Recognizing how past wounds, particularly from maternal relationships, shape your behaviors and connections.
- **Building Authentic Connections**: Learning to cultivate trust, set boundaries, and embrace vulnerability to form deeper relationships.
- **Strategies for Healing**: Implementing actionable steps like forgiveness, open communication, and mindfulness to move forward with clarity and purpose.

Action Steps Forward

Here's how you can keep the momentum going:

1. **Reflect Regularly**: Journaling isn't just for venting—it's a tool for understanding. Dedicate time to write about your progress, challenges, and victories. This helps you track growth and identify patterns that still need addressing.
2. **Connect with a Community**: Join support groups, therapy circles, or even online forums where people share similar experiences. There's strength in shared

stories, and sometimes hearing "me too" can be incredibly validating.
3. **Practice Mindfulness**: Engage in grounding activities like meditation, yoga, or even mindful walks. These practices help you stay present and reduce the stress of dwelling on the past or worrying about the future.

Activity: The Letter to Yourself

To solidify what you've learned, here's a simple but powerful exercise:

- Write a letter to yourself—your *past* self and your *future* self.
    - To your *past self*, offer forgiveness and understanding. Acknowledge the pain and the choices made, and remind yourself that it's okay to let go of the weight you've carried.
    - To your *future self*, outline your hopes and intentions. Describe the life you're building and the relationships you're nurturing. What does healed, authentic living look like for you?

This exercise isn't about perfection—it's about reflection. Revisit these letters when you need a reminder of how far you've come and where you're headed.

Acknowledging the Journey

Healing isn't linear, and it doesn't come with a set timeline. You might stumble; you might take steps backward. That's okay. What matters is that you keep moving forward, even when it's hard.

Remember, this book is a tool—not the whole toolbox. Therapy, continued self-discovery, and leaning on your support network are just as important. The key is to stay committed to your growth and to give yourself grace along the way.

Closing Thoughts

As you step out of these pages and back into the rhythm of your life, know this: you've already started rewriting your story. Every decision you make from here on out is a choice to prioritize healing, connection, and self-respect.

When old patterns resurface or new challenges arise, remember the tools you've gained. Choose understanding over resentment, vulnerability over fear, and hope over despair.

And when you need a little extra inspiration, reflect on this:

"The only real battle in life is between hanging on and letting go." — Shannon L. Alder

Every day, you have the chance to decide what to hold onto and what to release. Let that thought guide you as you move forward—lighter, freer, and more empowered.

Here's to your journey of healing, growth, and thriving—not just for a moment, but for a lifetime. You've got this.

One Final Prompt

As you close this book, ask yourself:

- *What's the first step I'll take today to reclaim my story?*
  Write it down. Commit to it. Then go make it happen.

www.ingramcontent.com/pod-product-compliance
Lightning Source LLC
Chambersburg PA
HW060507030426
7CB00015B/1784